PRAISE FOR THIS NEW TECHNIQUE:

"For years, I have sent my psychotherapy clients to Judith Hipskind. The insight they gain is of both spiritual and practical significance. The pictures in the hand reveal the truth of the soul as reflected in the body. The basic premise of Bioenergetic Analysis is that the body does not lie. The revelation of the metaphorical and literal stories in the hands can be a helpful support to the analysand in the search for the full and satisfying manifestation of self in this lifetime."

—Gay Mallon-Frank, M. A.
Certified Bioenergetic Therapist
Dallas, Texas

"When Judith Hipskind read my knuckles, a simple, stick-like warrior, economically defined by no more than two lines, emerged on my little finger, accompanied by a panther on a neighboring finger. As we gazed at these my mind slipped back through ages upon ages to the earliest people in earth: what creatures did their weather-worn fingers harbor? The petroglyphs, cave drawings, and hieroglyphs left behind by those people hauntingly mirror the creatures on my silent knuckles."

—Thomas Neil Grove, Ph.D.
Professor of Comparative Mythology
Framingham, Massachusetts

"Judith Hipskind gets as much out of knuckles as most palmists do from the whole palm. From knuckles alone, she can give an accurate description of a person's life path, past, present, and future. Having my knuckles read was a fascinating revelation of how the hand reflects an inner dimension of outward events to come."

—Diane Eichenbaum
Astrologer
New York, New York

"Lines and symbols, shadings and textures — to the gifted reader our knuckles reveal an intimate written history of our lives, and a startling view of our probable future. One evening Judith Hipskind worked with a group of professional people at a gathering hosted in my home. Each individual received a short reading. After comparing notes, the consensus was that each person experienced a feeling of wonder at the revelation of who they were and who they might become."

—William Urban
Stockbroker
Portland, Oregon

Learn Secret Knowledge of Your Future Now!

Odd as it may seem, you carry around the unconscious knowledge of all the possibilities in your future. What if you could access this unconscious knowledge?

You can! This new technique involves simple tools ... the knuckles on the back of your hands. Throughout your entire life, a whole world of information has been at your fingertips, just waiting to be decoded.

The keys to this system are simple. Each finger has a meaning! In this revolutionary book, you will discover these meanings and how they relate to every aspect of your life.

To understand how you are faring in each of these areas, you need only look at the knuckles. The appearance of the skin reveals your orientation to life. Are you primed for success or stress?

To interpret other visual signals, you will need another person to scan your knuckles for tiny lines that actually form little pictures! Tiny stick figures in your knuckles give insight into your progress in the world and the best path for you to follow to find happiness and fulfillment.

These stick figures and other symbols talk about now, next week, next month, and up to three years ahead! With this view of your prospects, you can plan practical strategies and stay on top of the changing issues in your life.

The New Palmistry adds another dimension to the science of palm reading. A miniature world is hiding in the knuckles, just waiting to be discovered!

About the Author

Judith Hipskind has studied palmistry since 1967. She works as a professional palmist in Dallas, Texas, and conducts private research and teaches. She is the author of *Palmistry: The Whole View.*

To Write to the Author

If you wish to contact the author or would like more information about this book, please write to the author in care of Llewellyn Worldwide, and we will forward your request. Both the author and the publisher appreciate hearing from you and learning of your enjoyment of this book and how it has helped you. Llewellyn Worldwide cannot guarantee that every letter written to the author can be answered, but all will be forwarded. Please write to:

Judith Hipskind
c/o Llewellyn Worldwide
P.O. Box 64383-352, St. Paul, MN 55164-0383, U.S.A.

Please enclose a self-addressed, stamped envelope or $1.00 to cover costs.
If outside the U.S.A., enclose international postal reply coupon.

Free Catalog from Llewellyn

For more than 90 years Llewellyn has brought its readers knowledge in the fields of metaphysics and human potential. Learn about the newest books in spiritual guidance, natural healing, astrology, occult philosophy and more. Enjoy book reviews, new age articles, a calendar of events, plus current advertised products and services. To get your free copy of *Llewellyn's New Worlds of Mind and Spirit,* send your name and address to:

Llewellyn's New Worlds of Mind and Spirit
P.O. Box 64383-352, St. Paul, MN 55164-0383, U.S.A.

THE
NEW
PALMISTRY

*How to Read the Whole Hand
and the Knuckles*

Judith Hipskind

1996
Llewellyn Publications
St. Paul, Minnesota 55164-0383, U.S.A.

FIRST EDITION
Third Printing, 1996

Cover Design: Christopher Wells
Illustrations: Linda Norton
Photographs: Patricia Tetens
Book Design and Layout: Jessica Thoreson

Library of Congress Cataloging-in-Publication Data
Hipskind, Judith.
      The new palmistry: how to read the whole hand
      and the knuckles / Judith Hipskind.
         p.   cm.
        ISBN 1-56718-352-2
        1. Palmistry. I. Title.
      BF921.H64   1993
      133.6–dc20   93-38438
                                  CIP

Llewellyn Publications
A Division of Llewellyn Worldwide, Ltd.
P. O. Box 64383, St. Paul, MN 55164-0383

Printed in the United States of America

**This book is dedicated to a special few
of the most important people who have
helped me on the path:**

To a literary father from long ago,
who speaks to me across the river of time

To my own mother, who by her life and her death,
encouraged me to write

To Carr, who helped me see into
other dimensions

To Anais, Eduardo, and Hugo,
who embraced the Great Work and its sacrifices

To Gerrie Anne, a childhood friend who has
inspired me every step of the way

To Jill, who found many ways to lighten
the work of giving birth to this book

ACKNOWLEDGEMENTS

First and foremost, I want to express my appreciation to all of my clients. Without each and every one of them this book could not exist, because working with my clients allowed me to develop the New Palmistry and to understand exactly how the knuckles work. Without their cooperation, interest, and enthusiasm, and answers to my innumerable questions about their lives, aimed at exploring the signifcance of the shape, color, and lines of their knuckles, I would not know what I know today. I thank everyone who has ever worked with me, particularly those who have been clients over a period of years and have kept me informed about developments in their lives pertinent to their readings.

Friends who have shared an interest in exploring many different aspects of palmistry have inspired me, and I am particularly grateful for the friendship of Gaye Annand in London, Pearl Medor in New York, and especially the late John Lindsay, who was a guiding force for many in this field.

I want to acknowledge, too, the pioneering spirit of Carl Llewellyn Weschcke, who has urged me to write books on palmistry, and who originally provided the opportunity for a public life in the field, and the opportunity for research that touches everything I know about hands today.

For their help in preparing this manuscript, I want to thank Dale Moses and Jill Ungerman, who read all the pages, made suggestions, and asked for clarification of certain concepts. Their interest and enthusiasm also encouraged me.

Finally, many thanks to those who had their hands photographed for this book, sharing the warriors and symbols in their knuckles: Elizabeth Cox, Dixie Curtis, Alice Ann and Megan Dailey, Kathleen Dean, Rose Delelio, Renee Evans, Lisa and James Harris, Allison Ingels, Deborah Luedtke, Kathleen Mc Cumber, Jean McCurdy, Jim Maher, Gay Mallon-Frank, Trudy Maslonka, and Jill and Jay Ungerman.

TABLE OF CONTENTS

Foreword

On October 22, 1992, Judith Hipskind spoke to our Society for the Study of Physiological Patterns about her work with a new version of palmistry, focusing on the knuckles. We were left enthralled by the discoveries which she outlined for us. We wanted to hear more than our one evening permitted, but of course had to wait for her book to be published. Now that her book is available, it will be enjoyed by all those competent hand readers and eager students who long for something as original as the well researched and totally innovative work now presented here.

We have the work of a pioneer in her field, yielding something so entirely rational and scientific as well as being part of the living scene. Frankly, the ideas shown in the knuckles always existed, just waiting for expression. Now the time is ripe for the curtain to be pulled on a hitherto unnoticed and undeveloped area of hand analysis, and this is just what Judith has accomplished.

Up to this time, palmists have concentrated on the palm of the hand. As Judith makes clear, this side of the hand is really the subjective view of life. The objective view—that is, who is important to us and influences our days and years—can be seen on the knuckles of the fingers. The knuckles tell an interesting tale.

We are given a condensed way of looking at the difference between the two sides of the hand: to think of the palm side as the *self,* and the back side as the *other.*

Finally, Judith says, "When we start our work with the knuckles you will see how clearly others' actions show up and how these actions affect your future." This angle of analysis, on such a concentrated level, is entirely new to palmistry. The prevalence of people and the weight of their influence on us warrants the view the back of the hand and the knuckles offer. You will not be able to wait to read these enthralling insights, which you can prove for yourself, applying the concepts found in this book to your own practice of palmistry.

Mary E. Anderson, President
Society for the Study of
Physiological Patterns
London, England

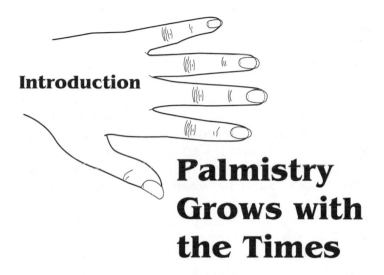

Introduction

Palmistry Grows with the Times

The world of palmistry is an adventure, and a very old one at that. One of the most marvelous features of palmistry is its adaptability. Palmistry has been speaking to people of their lives and loves from the earliest days of history until the present time. The message in the hands has adapted throughout history, addressing the concerns of all cultures and their times.

Today, a session with a palmist is more likely to resemble a therapy session than the mystical experience stereotypes suggest. The reality of palmistry today is that it has caught up with the times once again.

This book is meant to bring you up to date on what the hands have to offer today — a whole new world, waiting for exploration.

Before we begin, we must look at how stereotypes have affected the development of palmistry.

Although we have come a long way in the use of palmistry, it is unlikely that anyone would consider a session with a palmist to be at the same level as a meeting with a stockbroker or financial analyst.

There is good reason for this: most people do not know how much objective fact can be found in the hands, and the credibility gap between a recognized "professional" and a palmist is huge.

To account for this difference in the perceived value of a session between a professional and a palmist, let's look at a bit of the history of palmistry. Its ancient standing makes it a worthy candidate for a second glance.

Very few, if any, arts and sciences can be said to have come down to us from prehistory, with no exact account of their content, shape, or form. Palmistry and astrology are the two oldest studies of humankind, accounting for its behavior and its place in the universe. Astrology has the advantage of its tie with astronomy, a science, and the world of numbers. Palmistry has the distinct disadvantage of its association with charlatans; the mere mention of the words "the life line" brings on an instant anxiety about death, thanks to the reputation which that line has acquired. Many millennia of information and misinformation affect the state of palmistry today.

A stereotype today views palmistry as a tool of the Gypsies. This stereotype confuses the role of the Gypsies with charlatans. Gypsies with a true knowledge of the meaning of hands have kept palmistry alive, and we owe a lot of our present knowledge — and its survival through time — to them.

Throughout palmistry's history, some practitioners have been charlatans and dimmed its luster, giving it a fraudulent reputation that is undeserved.

Nothing that adapts to life and culture over several thousand years, and still has something to say, can be totally without value. We must understand how the reputation of palmistry became changed by association with Gypsies and charlatans.

An intelligent question about the spooky reputation of palmistry would be, "How did Gypsies' words in the past have such power?" The answer would undoubtedly be that their power stemmed from the fact that people in the Gypsies' heyday had much less control over their lives and events than we do today. In short, people were easier to manipulate and frighten by a few simple words than they are today, because life was often precarious.

When anyone has the power to change our lives, erasing all we have built with a few arbitrary decisions, we have reason to need reassurance. In older cultures, a chieftain's words, a king's temper, or a landlord's whims spelled the change of many a life in an instant. In an atmosphere like that, any inside knowledge would be eagerly sought.

Hard as it may be to believe, Gypsies were insiders once, renowned for their valuable power to see the future. The very king who might take away a person's lands for no good reason had every reason to cater to a Gypsy who could promise him that God would smile on his action and make the crops on the stolen land grow.

Gypsies were insiders because they were perceived to have a power of their own. Did they have such a power, or didn't they? We'll never know. We can only guess that some of their work was valid, because they were "in business" for so long. How long? From the beginning of time until the fall of the Holy Roman Empire. Not even Sears or Texaco can claim that hold on reality.

The Gypsies' last great stand was their employment with Charlemagne as spies for his organization. When the Holy Roman Empire fell, the Gypsies lost their last protectors, and their reputation never recovered as they were locked outside the city gates of Paris.

Is spying so unusual? Probably not to any industry in business today which keeps its products and their development under lock and key. Are we, in these technological days, so far removed from Gypsies' habits?

Technology today seems light years away from the era of Gypsies, and it is. What is startling to consider, however, is that their art was the height of technology in its day. And, even if we do not know how all the meanings for the features of the hands were developed, we do know that "necessity is the mother of invention." Palmistry was developed because it filled that need capably. The subject matter would not have hung around this long, even as a shadow of its former self — as it is today — unless it was needed. The Gypsies' reputation may have brought a lower profile to the subject, but did not completely erase the natural interest people have in the hands and their message.

Imagine the need for information in days before print, before cable television and satellites, before telephones! Now imagine that your hands have the very information you need encoded in them, in the form of lines and the shape of the hand itself. You would probably respond that this is taking things too far — that no matter how much you would want information, even under the pretense that no other form of communication existed — you could not imagine how or why your hands would have anything to say.

The startling fact is ... we are wired! Our nervous system is a communication center all in itself, sending and receiving messages that regulate everything we do and everything we are. That is the first fact. We are set up to be receptors of information through our nervous system.

The command center of that system, the brain, has a job to do, and that job is to ensure our survival. The brain does this by gathering information not only from cell to cell within the body, but from the environment that surrounds the body. We are programmed with reflexes to keep us out of direct physical danger, once we perceive it. We are also programmed to react to other types of threats, real or imagined, which could ultimately affect us, our survival, or the quality of our lives.

The brain is capable of monitoring our environment for more than the quick removal of our bodies from the path of a charging rhino or a truck out of control. The brain wants to know what the friendly or hostile influences are in every area of our lives.

We don't stop to think about this, and most of us don't realize that the brain prints a summary of what it learns in the course of doing its job of protecting us through the nervous system in our hands!

That is the secret of palmistry. Our world is revealed in our hands through the tiny records left by the action of the nerves on the palms' surface. The number of nerve endings in the hands is second only to the number in the brain itself. In a real sense, the hand is the brain's assistant. What the brain knows, the hands know, too — in capsule form. Just as a company manager's assistant knows enough to be of support.

During the days before our current technology, the hands were excellent "assistants," giving out information that the brain had somehow gathered about a person's prospects. And someone, somewhere, learned how to decode the hand's signals. That is perhaps no more remarkable than our attempts to decode signals from outer space today — a perfectly respectable scientific research project — because we have developed our planet to the limit and are seeking to expand our horizons.

Our knowledge grows. New products arrive, and new interpretations of old products emerge. We have only the remnants of the ancients' knowledge of the use of hands to broadcast the hands' information. We would not want to rework their knowledge because our world has changed. We appreciate Alexander Graham Bell's contribution and have moved on, adapting his invention to the needs of our times. The foundation of his work is still important, but applied differently. The foundation of palmistry is still with us today, and after years of obscurity, is now adapting itself to our times and needs.

Palmistry once belonged to rural people whose lives were tied to the seasons and cycles of nature. They had fewer options for the lifestyle choices we have today. Palmistry reflected this rhythm of existence with its emphasis on the major lines and blunt predictions. In their way of life, rural people knew everything had a cycle based on the seasons and the inescapable facts of life. Palmistry as a form of communication was tinged by a certain fatalistic style which matched their perception and experience of reality.

When the industrial age began, people flocked from their farms to the cities, the rhythms of life changed, and the number of choices grew. People felt the disorienting impact of new lifestyles. Jobs in this setting were crucial and not guaranteed. Vocational counseling came into vogue.

Palmistry, as a form of communication for meeting peoples' needs, gave advice about temperament and suitable jobs for each type, to help people cope.

And, as the stress of city life and its constant activity made people feel lost or alienated, disconnected from their former comforting reality, psychology began to take its place among the services offered to a growing segment of the population.

Palmistry adapted well, taking on the dress of modern psychology and losing much of its former emphasis on fatalistic predictions. As people recently awoke to the concept of "creating their own reality," modern palmistry stood available to help people understand themselves, their needs, and their choices.

What now? What is ahead for palmistry? The answer lies in the need to adapt to our shrinking world. In the space of a hundred years, people have made the transition from farm to city, and from life in a city to the global community.

The communication network that connects us all makes awareness of the world hard to shut out. The travel industry and corporate expansion keep us all on the move. The world is our back yard.

Our opportunities have grown at the same time as our world. To keep up, we now have to monitor world conditions. And we can do so, electronically, in the blink of an eye. Our condensed world and the territories of the globe are accessible in a way they never have been before.

How can palmistry meet the needs of these times? We need more than psychology and an analysis of our strengths to cope with today's developments. We need to know where to place ourselves, and when, on this tiny globe, to reach our maximum potential.

INTRODUCING THE NEW WORLD OF PALMISTRY

The amazing new form of palmistry has arisen to meet the needs of the day. Timing and mobility are two issues of paramount importance for anyone making decisions today. Choices are often so abundant that we have to be selective.

If we are offered a job in San Francisco and another in New York, and find we have no conscious basis for choosing one city over another — each city is an equally pleasing prospect, fulfilling career goals and social needs — how can we be sure we make the right decision? We would have a nagging feeling that one city ought to be a better choice, because logic tells us that no two cities could work out exactly the same in our lives.

Deep down, in an unconscious part of our mind, we seem to know the truth about the two cities, and which one holds the most potential for us. The part of our brain that constantly scans our territory (and any potential territory) has picked up the answer, and stored it away. Often this unconscious knowledge is what makes us act on impulse, on a "hunch," or on intuition. Acting on a hunch is not an irrational way to behave, but is simply movement toward a goal without conscious awareness.

Acting on a hunch is fun and acceptable when the matter involved is a small one — which movie to go to, which phone call to make next to make a sale — but when the stakes are as large as a whole lifestyle, most people would feel better having conscious reasons for their choices.

Now, what if we could get to the unconscious knowledge of the future we all hold inside, to help us make decisions? What if there were a key, or even just a few clues to guide us?

Think for a minute about all the clues your body gives out about your concerns. How you feel about a person or an event shows in your face, though you don't deliberately put the expression there. When you are tired, your shoulders begin to sag, though you don't realize it. If you are nervous or impatient, your fingers might begin to tap on an object near you, and only the noise they make as they strike that object makes you aware that you are moving your fingers. Tiny impulses from the brain have sent the message along to the outside of the body, where your reaction is visible.

In the case of the hands, impulses from the brain send their message out to the tips of the fingers, where the unconscious knowledge of the future is made visible. Looking at any part of the hand, the palm or the back of the hand, is very much like reading a computer printout. Information we would not otherwise have is made available.

The palm side of the hand has long been relied upon to give us facts and guidance about our lives. Now, in our new world of palmistry, we

can concentrate on a different area of the hand —
the knuckles!

The greatest secret to expanding the kind of
information a hand can give lies in using the back
of the hand to view our world. Research has shown
that the back side of the hand represents the world
around us, the people and places in it, and their
significance for us.

In this world full of people and places, we all
have a "spot in the sun," a place where we can
more easily fulfill our potential through the opportunities offered to us.

New palmistry concentrates, then, on choices
and how best to make them through a new way to
see people and places quickly. Since we do not
have years to spend as we make career, family,
and lifestyle choices, the new system includes timing that is more immediate than that which standard palmistry offers. That system looks at time in
terms of years of one's life. New palmistry can
judge events and circumstances in terms of
months, weeks, and occasionally, days!

All of this information is available on the back
side of the hand, through the new meanings given
to the fingers, the time frame given to each hand
and set of knuckles, and through the startling
images that are formed in the knuckles.

We have a whole new world of palmistry to discover! And more of the world that surrounds us,
for the new palmistry includes a system of designating countries, states, and cities in the knuckles!

Read on — you will be entertained, and find
that this new view of the hands has much to offer
you as you explore your world and its choices
more closely.

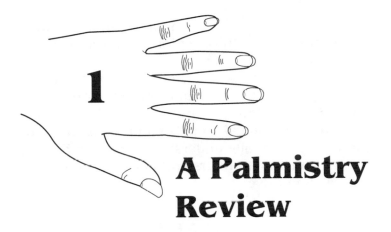

1

A Palmistry Review

One tiny palm, one large world of information! For those who have read books on palmistry, do you remember how the palm's illustrations often look busy, and impossible to decipher?

Such illustrations, while a bit confusing, are proof of the great amount of information enclosed in the small space of a palm. As a graphic record of a person's potential, a palm has to cover a lot of territory: details from all the stages of life, starting with birth, continuing through childhood, education, career, marriage, children, advances in life, and assorted events.

Through its current format, palmistry has done a very good job of providing guidance in all these areas and as a basis for understanding the whole person. Palmistry reveals a person's character, energy, needs, and talents, and notes the challenges that can arise in the course of a lifetime.

Let's look for a moment at how palmistry processes all this information, using its standard categories of interpretation.

The main categories used to define the hands' meanings are shape, length, color, mounts, and lines. The first four features provide a solid background for the lines' tantalizing information about the future. To really understand a person's potential, we must first understand his or her character, energy, and drive.

SHAPE

Shape is the first feature used in palmistry to define a person's behavior and motivation. Shape is analyzed first from the palm itself, then from the fingertips and nails.

The palm has three possible shapes: round, square, and flared. Each palm has at least one of these shapes, and often a combination of them. Each shape has its own set of characteristics.

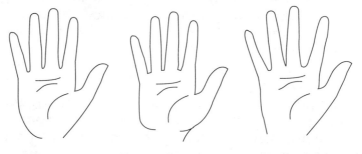

Round   Square   Flared

Palm shapes

Flared

Round

Square

Pointed

Fingertip shapes

A round palm reveals a warm, friendly, optimistic person who wants to enjoy life; a square palm means a person who is oriented to the "bottom line" in any discussion, and one who wants good value in return for time and money spent. A flared (traditionally called spatulate) palm person wants excitement and adventure.

Fingertips have four distinct shapes: flared, square, round, and pointed. Fingertip shape shows our instinctive approach to life and what use of our energy satisfies us.

Flared fingertip people are dynamos. They must keep on the move, and they feel that their actions must make an impact. They are the least quiet of the four types. Square fingertip people are conscientious, detail-oriented, and must feel they are creating order with their actions. Round fingertip types like people and must have a social life.

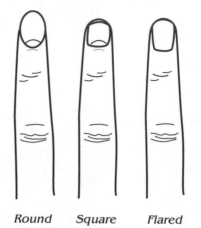

Round   Square   Flared

Fingernail shapes

Pointed tip people are a bit paradoxical. They are open and receptive, but they are not often easily led down a path not of their own choosing. They need to act on their own terms.

Fingernails have three different shapes: round, square, and flared. Only the sides and the base of the nail count in this category; the manicured part of the nail is not used to determine shape. Nail shape reveals how a person will interact with others.

Round nail people are intuitive and adaptable, and will give everyone a fair chance, while square nail types are perfectionists, demanding a lot of others, and giving much in return. Flared nail types are restless, curious, and motivated to try anything new.

Apart from the shapes above, the palms and the nails can be analyzed for another type of shape: width and narrowness. The wider the nails and palm, the greater the energy the person has.

Physically fit, wide nail or palm people can take on the world, and create quite a stir in their surroundings. Narrow nails and palms show a quieter, more reserved type whose energy is not as naturally high and must be conserved and applied at a steady, moderate pace.

One last application of shape applies to palms alone: thick or thin. Thick, fleshy palms reveal an astounding amount of energy. They belong to people who are out in the world, and "in your face." These are the people who show up in the papers, mostly as promoters, developers, and politicians. Thin, delicate-looking palms belong to the world's creative dreamers. Just give these people plenty of space and time to do their own thing. The depth of their perceptions and sympathy can surprise and nurture their friends and loved ones.

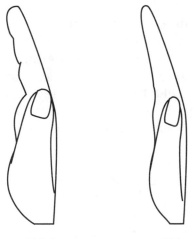

Thick   *Thin*

Palm thickness

LENGTH

Length is the next feature used to decipher character, energy, personality, and approach to life. Length is applied to the palm, to the fingers, and to the thumb, as well as the nails.

First, palm length. How flexible a person is, how open to change, is revealed by the length of the palm. A short palm, as wide as it is long, means a person adjusts quickly to change and takes life in stride. A long palm, longer that it is wide, shows a nature that is somewhat resistant to change.

Finger length is measured by the longest finger on the hand, which should be three-quarters as long as the palm. Shorter or longer than that mark defines the length. Finger length is a quick guide to a person's temperament and ability to handle details.

Short fingers mean that the person is a real live wire! These people are enthusiastic and want to "wing it," skipping the details of life in the moment and grasping the big picture. People with long fingers take their time. They move slowly, analyzing each detail, making sure of everything in their path — whether it is their husband or wife, or their job.

The thumb is a special case, standing apart as it does on the hand. Its length is measured against the side of the hand; held close to the index finger, the tip should come halfway up the bottom section of the index finger. Longer or shorter than that mark defines the length.

Thumb length reveals decision-making ability. Long thumbs are the strong ones, deflecting all opposition and challenges and persisting on their self-determined course. Short thumbs show personalities that often defer to others' wishes. These people are the diplomats who keep life smooth for those in their midst.

Nail length relates to temperament and health. For length, the nails are again only measured from the base up to the part where the manicure begins.

Short nail people are doers, realistic in their outlook. Long nails often belong to dreamers, people who are artistic and visionary at heart. People with short nails can be short on patience, while those with long nails can have the patience of a saint. Each nail length gives a special view of health, but the typical palmist will only use this feature to talk about the quality and type of energy a person has. Health diagnosis is best left to doctors and other medical experts.

COLOR

Color is one of the wonders of palmistry. Color acts as a virtual biofeedback indicator, showing health, happiness, enthusiasm, and motivation; or the opposite qualities, a dull and withdrawn nature, being "asleep at the wheel," along with health difficulties — which sometimes cause the last traits to spring into existence!

Color comes and goes in the hands, and is analyzed in both the palms and the nails. Mostly, color remains the same, but it can change at a moment's notice. A traumatic event brings on a white color in the hands, just as it does in the face.

A moment of surprise or joy and happiness can cause a pink flush in the hands. Good health also produces a pink color. The longer lasting colors in the hands are indicators of a person's mindset and motivations.

Color is used to describe both physical and psychological patterns. In palmistry, pink is the preferred color, showing good health and abundant energy and motivation. Rather like the phrase "in the pink of things," this color means a person feels upbeat and perceives life to be good. A pale or white color in the palm or nails always denotes a lower physical energy, and at times a lack of motivation and outgoing qualities as a result of the lower energy. The energy turns inward. This is not always negative. Many creative people who concentrate on an inner world, like artists and writers, have a pale tone to the skin.

Other colors are associated with health matters. A yellow tinge in the palm, or a blue or purple color in the nails, relates to certain health conditions.

The most interesting use of color is that pink — there is usually some pink to be found in the palm, in the lines, or somewhere — will confirm the areas of progress and strength in a person's life. Color can be used to spot potential that is actively in use, for often only certain areas of the hand are pink. Qualities that are actively being used to enhance a life produce a pink color; times of stress, of just getting by on "automatic pilot," bring on a paler color to the palm.

MOUNTS

With the mounts we come closer to the heart of palmistry: the bumps on the palm, followed by the lines. With both mounts and lines we concentrate exclusively on the palm's surface, while the features of shape, length, and color apply to the fingers and nails as well as the palm.

Mounts are the little raised areas on the palm's surface. The entire surface is not flat, but curved in spots where the contours, called mounts, stand out. These contours define the personality and potential abilities, just as a desert or mountain defines a physical setting and the activities appropriate to it.

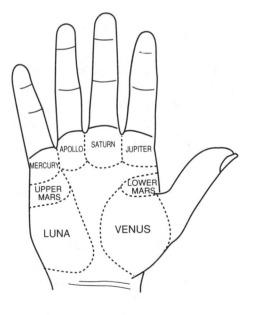

Mounts

The mounts and lines work together in a good hand analysis. Lines pass through or around the mounts and the mounts themselves have small lines on them. The mounts describe talent and drive that feeds into the lines and in turn activates their potential.

Each mount has a name symbolic of the energy it represents. There are seven mounts associated with seven different types of personalities and approaches to life.

Mount	Approach to Life
Jupiter	Leader
Saturn	Thinker
Apollo	Creator
Mercury	Entrepreneur
Venus	Lover
Mars	Fighter
Luna	Dreamer

Mounts are a great guide to energy, motivation, and talents. They are a key to understanding career potential. The best developed mount in the hands is a key to a person's "type" and the abilities associated with that type. To determine which mount is the best, pick the mount that stands up highest and is firm to the touch.

Here are a few traits and career options for each mount.

Mount	Traits	Career Potential
Jupiter	Ambition, strong ego, desire for achievement	Lawyer, politician, teacher, speaker, diplomat, administrator

Mount	Traits	Career Potential
Saturn	Serious, logical, concerned with balance, observant	Analyst, scientist, mathematician, geologist, farmer, metallurgist, ecologist
Apollo	Joyous, attracts friends, loves music, beauty, and drama	Artist, art gallery owner, arts and crafts creator, film, video, music, designer, make-up artist, image consultant
Mercury	Quick mind, insightful, good money manager, intellectual	Businessman, entrepreneur, advisor, speaker, psychiatrist, internist, banker
Venus	Affectionate, peacemaker, love of luxury, strong feelings for home	Beauty and fashion industries, music, dance and theater, day care provider, teacher, marriage counselor, social planner, family therapist
Lower Mars	Loves a challenge, wants to prove abilities, has initiative	Athletics, outdoor recreation planner, firefighter, surgeon, paramedic, founder of small businesses

Mount	Traits	Career Potential
Upper Mars	Very patient, persevering, dependable, steady, calm, courageous, nutures others	Arts, crafts, heavy equipment sales, communications manufacturing and production, air traffic controller, engraving, management
Luna	Romantic, poetic, idealistic, love of travel and languages, psychic	Linguist, travel consultant, pilot, transportation industry, poet, writer, detective, import/export businesses

The mounts paint a picture of natural ability and potential which is further explained by the path the lines take.

LINES

Lines tell quite a tale, walking us through the story of our lives from birth to the end of our days. They speak of our activated potential, in contrast to our constant potential seen in the mounts. Lines tell "what's happening," both in the present and for the future; they record past events and conditions which leave their mark on us.

With lines, we are, in effect, "telling time." Lines let us see the past, present, and future as distinct increments; that is their special function. Three main lines are used to decipher time in the hand: the life line, the fate line, and the head line. Occasionally, the heart line and the Apollo or Mercury lines are consulted for their input, usually as a back-up to verify the data in the main lines.

Lines really do tell it all, describing our heredity, our birth, our childhood, early and later education, the beginning of our careers, the progress we make, the challenges we find, and our mates, children, and lifestyle.

There is a basic pattern of information available from each line. The markings and appearance

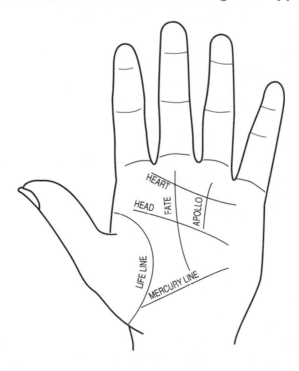

Lines

of the line itself gives further details. But for this review, we will simply look at the type of details each line presents.

Life Line

Reveals the conditions of birth, relationship with parents, results of early and later education, first experience with the working world, and subsequent chances for success. Opportunities for expansion, promotions, travel, and change of residence can be seen.

The line faithfully records events which shape a life, the joys and sorrows, successes and challenges. The line also describes physical strength and prospects for health.

In addition, the life line is the first and main line used to "tell time." Time on the line is set up from birth through age eighty or beyond, in one-year increments. Any year of a life can be pinpointed.

Heart Line

Reveals the full range of emotions, the chances for happiness in home and private life, the ability to give and receive love; defines emotional needs and describes how they can best be met.

The heart line is another major source of health information, as the "heart" in this case is both figurative and literal. This line gives clues to the circulation and mineral levels in the body.

Head Line

Describes how the mind works. Is the person imaginative or practical? Clear-thinking or fuzzy-headed? Able to concentrate or scattered? This line gives clues to attention span, type of interests that would fulfill a person, as well as abilities to be used for success.

Fate Line

This line has come to be known by such a glamorous term, and a rather mysterious sounding one. A moment's thought might reveal that everyone has a destiny of some sort; the only way to fulfill it is to forge ahead with conscious effort. The fate line is really a work line. The line reveals one's orientation to life, and one's level of involvement and commitment to all parts of life — family, work, friends, fun, and social activities. The line shows a desire to make a difference. Absence of a fate line can mean a drifter or one who does not believe in his or her ability to make a mark with a contribution to life. Fate lines are typically found in three or more sections spread across the palm, reflecting the different directions a life can take.

Time is also figured on this line, from the wrist to the top of the hand.

Apollo Line

The Apollo line is a plus! After the work and direction shown by the life, head, heart, and fate lines, this line reflects time, energy, and talent "left over," or a need for further outlets. People with an Apollo line are a cut above average, standing out with their personalities and talents — and desire to share them. Most artists, performers, and public figures have well-developed Apollo lines. So do people whose lives are private; they are satisfied with their lives and chances to connect with people in their community.

Mercury Line

This line means business — literally. Although the Mercury line is small in size compared to the other lines, it is, like the fate line, an anchor to success. This is because a good Mercury line signifies a sound body, an unworried mind, and a flair for business and negotiating. The senses and perceptions are sharper, intuition keener; life can quickly fall into place for the person who has a strong Mercury line.

All these features in a palm make it a rich source of interpretation when meanings are found for them:

1. Size, shape, and length applied to the palm, the fingertips, and the nails.

2. The mounts, their marks, their consistency and color.

3. The lines, their depth, direction, marks, and color.

The world of the palm is fascinating, and leads to the discovery of yet another world on the back side of the hand.

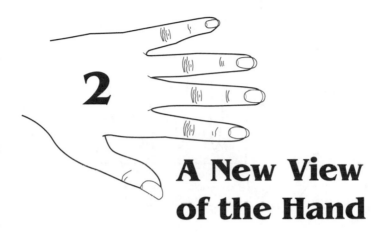

2

A New View of the Hand

To analyze the hands thoroughly, palmistry traditionally divides the palm into little sections that treat different areas of a person's life and psyche. One good example of this division is the well-established view of the Three Worlds of Palmistry.

These worlds were borrowed from the ancient concept of dividing reality into three sections: heaven, earth, and hell.

The bottom third of the hand, the heel of the hand, represents "hell," or our physical and material needs. The middle section of the hand reflects "earth," or our emotional and social lives; the top section of the hand, the fingers, is associated with "heaven," or our spiritual and intuitive lives.

Such divisions are useful when we are sizing up the various parts of the hand. Prior to now, "of the hand" meant "of the palm." The back side of the hand has not been used to predict events, only to define health (from the nails) and certain personality characteristics (from the size and length of the fingers, skin texture, and other clues).

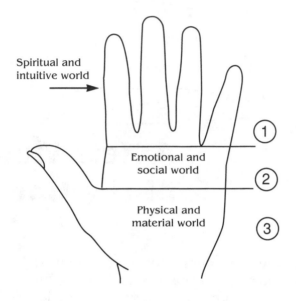

Spiritual and
intuitive world

Emotional and
social world

Physical and
material world

The Three Worlds of the palm

So much is happening in the world today, that
to keep up with events we have to develop the territory of the hand, if the hands are to reflect reality
adequately. In our new system, the area available for
interpretation has expanded to include the knuckles
and other features on the back of the fingers.

Expanding the territory of the hand to be analyzed makes possible the distinction of the two
worlds in the view of the new palmistry. In our system, the palm represents one world, and the back
of the hand, another world. We are going to learn
the difference between these worlds as a key to
understanding the reality the new palmistry reflects.

THE TWO WORLDS OF THE HAND

The palm represents our personal world, starting with our birth and moving through our childhood, education, career, marriage, our own children, and our future prospects.

The back side of the hand represents the world that surrounds us, and the people and conditions in it that affect our potential during every waking minute.

The view from the palm side of the hand is a more stately panorama, given over to a span of eighty years of potential living. The outlook of the back side of the hands is quick and succinct, summing up our relevant past experience, with people and conditions around us, and projecting ahead to a maximum of three years in the future.

The palm reveals people in our lives who are extensions of the self: parents, mates, and children. Add ancestors and grandchildren to that view, if you like, for they are just further reaches of the self.

The back side of the hand speaks of anybody who has a potential impact on our lives: a sibling, a best friend, a teacher, a boss, an acquaintance, even a stranger. The back of the hand reflects the world around us; that world is mostly made of people.

The palm side of the hand reflects conditions that we can control, experiences we can process and put to use, goals we can set, and determination and will that we can muster to establish a large part of our reality.

The back side of the hand reflects the things we cannot control: our boss' mood, the economy, whether or not the sun is shining.

We can also apply these terms to the two sides of the hand: the palm side reflects subjective reality; the back side, objective reality.

We can take the matter the palm represents, our opportunity plus the use of our will, and make it what we want. What we do about our lives is a subjective decision, and can make a difference in our reality. But, because whatever we think or hope or wish for does not alter the reality revealed by the back of the hand, its nature could be called objective.

Here is a list that sums up the differences between the two sides of the hand.

The palms reflect:	The backs reflect:
Our personal world	The "real" world
People who are extensions of the self	People in our lives
Subjective reality	Objective reality
Events and conditions over which we have some control	Events and conditions we cannot control

A very condensed way of looking at the difference between the two sides of the hand is to think of the palm side as the self, and the back side as the other.

In this view, all your behavior and accomplishments are recorded on the palm side of the hand, while the behavior and accomplishments of others are revealed on the back side.

Palm shows:	Back of hand shows:
Your world	Others' worlds
Your hopes	Others' hopes
Your goals	Others' goals
Your inspiration	Others' inspiration
Your motivation	Others' motivation
Your talents	Others' talents
Your temperament	Others' temperament
Your health	Others' health
Your expectations	Others' expectations
Your future	Others' future

When we start our work with the knuckles you will see how clearly others' actions show up, and how these actions affect your future.

This angle of analysis, on such a concentrated level, is entirely new to palmistry. The prevalence of people, and the weight of their influence on us, warrants the view the back of the hands and knuckles offer.

PEOPLE IN OUR LIVES

To underscore the importance of our daily contact with others, and as a preview to appreciating the world of the knuckles, let's think about the people in our lives.

If you were to visualize your world for a moment, what would you see? Your job? Your marriage? Your family? Your schooling? Whatever makes up your world, none of it will take place without one important piece of the puzzle — people! Even if you only "see" the house you own or the condo you rent when you visualize your world, and you live alone, there are still people involved. You have either a banker and a mortgage, or a landlord.

Your world is made of people. How do you buy your groceries or pay for gas for your car? Through people. When you go to a movie, who's on the screen? People. At a concert or play, who's on stage and in the audience? People, that's who.

Unless you are in an unlikely situation — a hermit, growing your own food, raising your own cattle, living in total isolation, in your own hut, on your own land, in your own woods — you must come into contact with others.

People smooth the way for us. People we know well enhance our lives more significantly than a brief interaction with the grocery store clerk or gas station attendant. But these people affect us, too. A cheerful hello can send us on our way with a smile. A grouchy, gruff exchange can bring us down. And as for people at a distance, movie characters can inspire us, or thrill us. Actors on the stage can do the same. The people sitting in the audience emit their own particular energy, contributing to what we perceive as the "atmosphere" of a place.

The sum total of the energy put out by everyone we come into contact with affects us. The impact is cumulative and mostly operates on an unconscious level.

You do not go around thinking, "Oh, it just took another person to make my day. I've got my gas paid for, and now I'll deal with the woman at the dry cleaners, before I go to the hardware store and ask that friendly fellow to find those brackets."

Every person you meet along the way counts. Your brain keeps track, both sequentially, recording your reality as you move through your day; and by association, as your brain tries to put all your experiences into a slot that creates a kind of completion to the rag-tag events of the day.

People define our everyday reality. We are going to give them their due when we find them in our knuckles with the stories they have to tell us.

DEFINING THE BACK OF THE HAND

Now we are ready to consider what exactly we mean by the "back of the hand" in new palmistry. The area we normally mean when speaking of the back of the hand is not included in this new form of palmistry. We will not use the whole back of the hand, but only the fingers and knuckles. The ordinary back of the hand does not have the features to explore that the fingers and knuckles do.

With this special view of the back of the hand, limited to the fingers from the point where they

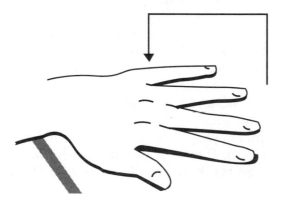

join the hand down to the tips, we have a minia-ture world just waiting to be explored.

A New Glance at the Finger Sections

The whole length of the finger sections means something. Each section can reveal details about our lives and our needs. However, the entire area of the finger is not equal in its ability to yield informa-tion for interpretation. Look closely at the back of your fingers, and you will see that the longer con-necting sections between the knuckles do not have many — or sometimes, any — lines on them. These longer finger sections, called phalanges, do have color, shape, and texture, but no lines to speak of.

Size and Shape of Knuckles

The knuckles are the center of the system because their features yield the most information. The first thing we must do is define "knuckles" in our new system. Modern palmistry looks at knuck-les, but the view refers to the knuckle under the skin. Modern palmistry wants to know if the knuckle itself is very bony and enlarged, or smooth. Arthritis affects the shape of knuckles in this view. But without the influence of arthritis, some knuckles are smoother than others. Large knuckles in modern palmistry mean that you can feel the bone and cartilage under the skin as little protuberances.

In this new system of palmistry, we never refer to the size of the knuckles under the skin, but we do analyze the knuckles for size and shape. If we aren't using the bones as a point of reference, what are we looking at? The skin itself!

Shape of the Skin Covering the Knuckles

Look again at your knuckles, the middle ones. Notice the skin on them. Is it smooth? Is it bunchy-looking, with raised ridges? Some knuckles with raised ridges look like a circle, others take on a square appearance. Most raised ridge knuckles simply have an individual appearance, unique according to the way the skin is raised.

The knuckles are not a blank space, but have their own unique shape: the way the skin covers the area, and a distinct pattern of lines.

Look harder at those knuckles and begin to appreciate how distinctive they look. One might be smooth, and one might have raised ridges. If more than one knuckle has raised ridges, then each of those can have a different shape.

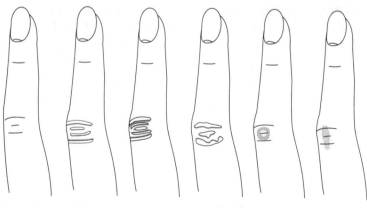

| Smooth | Raised | Raised/ firm | Raised/ soft | Dented | Furrowed |

Knuckle shapes

The tip knuckles, nearer the nails, have some variations in shape, though less than the middle knuckles.

Color in the Knuckles

One of the most fascinating features of the knuckles is the little-recognized fact that each knuckle has a potentially different distribution of color. The shades of color on a knuckle are subtle, not glaring, in their appearance.

A person would have to be very odd indeed to go around thinking, "My knuckles are different colors!" But they are. If your skin is white, then you can have shades of pink, ranging from a faint blush to a deep and vivid pink. The knuckles can also be pale, whiter by contrast than the rest of the surrounding skin.

If your skin is dark, you will still have contrasting areas of color on your knuckles. Parts of a knuckle will be darker, others not as dark, as the pigment appears to pool on the knuckle. Your skin will also have a shine and sheen on it that is more noticeable than the shine on lighter skin.

In the chapters on color in the knuckles, we will find out the significance of these color variations. For now, just be aware that you have them. If you look closely at your knuckles, particularly the middle ones, you will in most cases find subtle color differences along the surface.

Lines on the Knuckles

Now look again at the knuckles. What do you see? Lines, lots of them. You can count horizontal lines. They are the most noticeable, and any artist drawing a full-scale hand would include these horizontal lines in the picture.

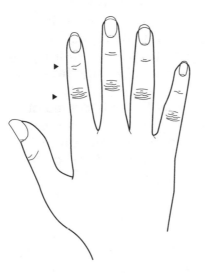

As you can see, the middle knuckles have several horizontal lines, and the tip knuckles in the drawing are usually represented by one or two horizontal lines. Many hands in real life have only one deep line at the tip knuckle. Others have several, tinier lines in front and in back of the main lines.

In standard palmistry, no special emphasis is given to the surface of the knuckles, to the skin's shape, or color lines. Nor to the following amazing feature.

Warriors in the Knuckles

The real secret to the heart of the knuckles' world is the existence of tiny figures which look just like warriors! Until now, their appearance in the knuckles seems to have gone unnoticed.

These warriors are drawn like stick figures, in a variety of poses. Each figure's posture tells a tale, much like a mime conveying a point without words. Their posture is dynamic and action-oriented. Because they symbolize action, it is possible to decode a story from their posture to apply to the life of the person on whose knuckles they appear.

A warrior may look victorious or discouraged, aggressive or defensive, exultant or secretive; it may appear to be standing still or leaping about, strong or weak. (Illustrations of these postures can be found on page 217.)

We will learn much more about the warriors and their discovery. We will also read about the discovery of other figures and symbols in later chapters.

For now, we are just at the dawn of our awareness that there is something very different about the back of the hand and the features it offers for interpretation.

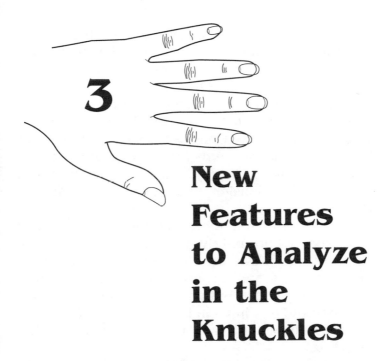

New Features to Analyze in the Knuckles

The figures in the knuckles, the warriors, are a wonderful fact of nature. It is truly incredible to realize that all the tiny, fine lines in the knuckles are capable of organizing themselves into images. No one would have imagined that such a small area could be hiding information, reduced to a scale that challenges the eye intent on perceiving them.

A few of the images are nearly as large as the knuckle itself; other images are only a fraction of the knuckle in height. The lines that make up the images vary in depth, so that a minute or two of concentrated attention is necessary to make the images come into focus.

Spotting the first image is anyone's moment of triumph. It only gets easier after that initial achievement to perceive more and more of the amazing world of images in the knuckles.

You won't become a believer, most likely, until you have seen your first image. Then, watch out! You may get hooked and want to spend all your time looking at the hands (and knuckles!) of everyone you know. And, truly, the more you do see in knuckles, the easier working with them will become.

When you first look at knuckles, what can you expect? Fortunately, you do not have to concentrate right away on the images they contain, because there are two other features to analyze first. Both of these features are much more obvious than the tiny lines in the knuckles. These two features consist of the shape and color in the knuckles.

Although the interpretation of the knuckles forms a new approach to palmistry, the features that can be analyzed are a miniature version of the way any palm is interpreted.

To work with a palm, we look at shape, color, lines, and the texture and consistency of the palm. We will use exactly the same factors to analyze the knuckles, in approximately the same order.

Analyzing a palm, we usually first note the shape of the palm and fingers, then the color; and then the lines, texture, and consistency.

Working with the knuckles, we will note the shape and color, then look for the lines. And if there is a special consistency to the knuckles, this will have a meaning. Consistency refers to the degree of softness or firmness in an area we are looking over. For a contrast in consistency, think of the difference between custard and a raw carrot. One is soft, the other firm. Texture refers to the quality of the skin on the knuckle, which may be smoother or rougher, by contrast.

Next we will discuss what to look for in a knuckle.

SHAPE

This is the appearance of the skin covering the knuckle. Each knuckle can be flat and smooth, or have raised ridges. The raised ridges can be soft or firm. A knuckle can also be found with the opposite of a raised ridge, and show a dent instead. The last type of shape to be found in a knuckle is a furrow. A furrow is an oblong-shaped depression which looks like a rut, or a trough.

Here is a list of the possible shapes we will work with.

1. Smooth ridges
2. Raised ridges
   a. Soft
   b. Firm
3. Dented ridges
4. Furrows

Illustrations of these shapes can be found on page 25.

COLOR

No knuckle is all one color. There will be slight variations in the skin tone, ranging from very pink to very pale. This is true for white hands. In people of color, the knuckles will have combinations of even and uneven shading in the pigment. Some areas of the knuckle will be darker than the others, and the skin will have a high degree of shine to it.

Here is a quick preview of what color in the knuckles means.

A pink tone on white hands, and the shine on dark hands, is an extremely important signal: a GO! Wherever the knuckles want to give good news, you will find a pink tone, or a shine. When the knuckles want to signal a slow-down or a challenge, the color becomes reduced, very pale, on white hands; darker on dark hands. In other words, under stress, the white on white knuckles becomes whiter, and the dark areas on dark knuckles become darker.

The real key to analyzing the knuckles is to get an accurate idea of the different tones and shades on the skin, because color "colors" the whole story that the lines and shape reveal. We will later see how this works in Chapters 14 and 15, on color, and in the sample readings in Chapter 20.

On white hands watch for:	On dark hands watch for:
Bright pink	Lighter pigment
Pale pink, like a blush	Average skin tone, matching overall skin
Average skin tone	Darker pigment
White or pale tone, or stark white	Shiny areas

LINES

The middle knuckles have the largest number of lines to analyze. There are lines on the tip knuckles, just not as many, simply because the area of these knuckles is smaller. The raised ridges and greater amount of flesh on the middle knuckles will hold more lines than the smoother, smaller tip knuckles.

On the middle knuckles of both hands, we find tiny lines that run vertically, which are not the obvious horizontal lines.

What appear to be scratchy little lines running up and down on the knuckle, at first glance (Diagram A), turn out to be, in many cases, stick figures and other symbols (Diagram B). The tip knuckles also have these images.

Note that here, for the first time, we find the hands in the diagrams in an upside down position. This is the way the images face, outwards, and away from the person on whose hands they are found; in order to study the images, we have to look at them from the perspective in which they are found, to be accurate.

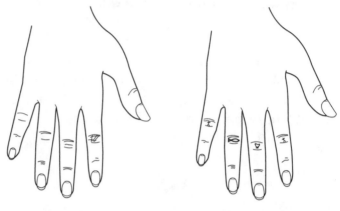

Diagram A   Diagram B

On the tip knuckles, there is a horizontal line that matters (Diagram C), right at the juncture where the knuckle bends. We will study that line in Chapter 6, as a mark indicating timing. The point is, a horizontal line on the tip knuckle is significant, though this is not the case with the middle knuckles, which are composed of many horizontal lines (Diagram D).

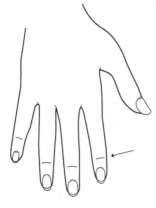

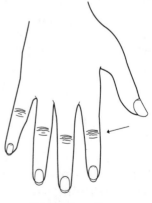

Diagram C   Diagram D

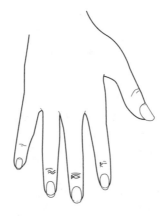

Diagram E

Other tiny lines are also found on the tip knuckles, as well as symbols and more stick and cartoon figures (Diagram E).

The lines on the knuckles are a bit more complex in nature than the lines on the palm. On the palm, a line is a line. On the knuckles, a line may be a line, a stick figure, a fully drawn figure, or a symbol. In other words, the lines on the knuckles are, most of the time, pictures, which is quite different from the way lines on the palm look.

The lines on the knuckles fall into two categories: figures and symbols. Figures are drawings of a human figure, whether the figure is etched as a stick figure, such as children draw, or as a fully drawn figure, such as the ones in cartoons.

A figure is always just one item, a human being, drawn in one of two basic ways. A symbol is different, for a symbol can be nearly any other type of drawing in the knuckle that is not a human figure. A symbol can be the drawing of an animal or a geometric shape or a piece of scenery, such as a cloud, mountain, or ocean.

To summarize the types of lines in knuckles:

1. Figures
   a. Stick figures, called "warriors"
   b. Fully drawn figures, looking like cartoon characters
2. Symbols
   a. Animals
   b. Geometric shapes
   c. Scenery

CONSISTENCY

All the middle knuckles are made of a series of ridges, divided by the obvious horizontal lines. This "accordion" effect of the skin on the knuckles gives the skin room to expand as the knuckles bend and fold. When the fingers are extended, some knuckles look smooth, while the skin on others appears to be bunched up. This means the ridges are raised. Any raised ridge will have its own consistency, and be soft or firm to the touch. An illustration of raised ridges is on page 25. Each of these types has a meaning, and the chapters on knuckle shape will explore the meanings in detail.

To check for consistency, then, look for raised ridges, and touch them to determine if they are soft or firm to the touch.

TEXTURE

The skin on both the tip and middle knuckles ordinarily resembles the skin on the rest of the fingers and the back of the hand. But occasionally, the skin on the knuckles looks pearlized or like leather. Although every skin by definition has a certain texture, in this system of palmistry, the word "texture" means something noticeably out of the ordinary, an added quality, on the surface of the skin.

The key to all these features in the knuckles is that they are tiny, and take getting used to; the effort merits a reward and pays returns in giving a whole new world of information.

Working with the knuckles can be the beginning of one of the greatest adventures in communication, a means to understand the influence of the world on each person, and a way to decipher just what each person will make of the world around him or her.

The knuckles may be small, but they are dynamic! They pack quite a punch with their tightly condensed information.

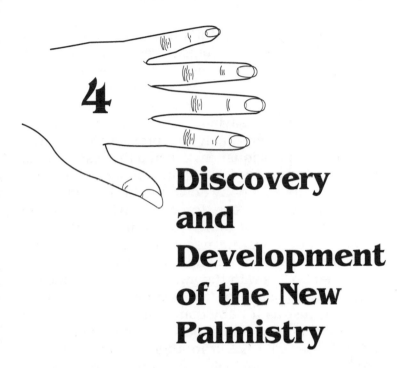

4

Discovery and Development of the New Palmistry

Knuckles! What in the world are the knuckles, and what do they have to do with our ordinary view of palmistry? Why are we looking at knuckles? These are perfectly understandable questions.

If you were to fully realize all the knuckles can do, you would have even more questions: HOW, would be the main one; how can the knuckles do what they do? And another: WHY? Why hasn't anyone discovered them before now?

Ten years of work went into answering the first question, how the knuckles can tell us what they do; a reply to the second question, why hasn't anyone discovered them before now, does not exist. That is unknown.

A good guess, and it's anybody's guess, why the revelation of the knuckles has sat in the wings waiting for discovery, is because, in the context of yesterday's culture, there was no pressing need for the material.

You know the saying, "necessity is the mother of invention." Very likely the pressure of today's developing consciousness pushed the discovery of knuckles forward; a force quite similar to the pressure that moves a baby down the birth canal.

Just because the force is invisible to the naked eye, and not under the control of the conscious mind, does not negate its action. And in a further comparison, a baby is born simply because it is time. So it is with the awareness of knuckles in palmistry. It is time for this awareness to surface.

And just as a baby comes from its mother, a part of her flesh and blood, the creation of the knuckle material has a mother, the palmistry we already know. That palmistry is the parent of the knuckle material, and in this stage, knuckles are a miniature copy of the "mother palmistry," sharing many of its characteristics.

Again, similar to a newborn baby, with inborn potential waiting to be developed, the new knuckle material will "grow up" and acquire a consciousness, a will, and a direction all its own. Many uses can be made of this material. We cannot predict at this moment what the fully-grown child will look like. We only know its "parentage," an already established body of knowledge, which is certainly a clue to the future development of our infant.

In time, knuckles will have the capability of doing all that the parent material does, and more.

The knuckle material will be shaped by the needs of the day in its coming of age, and will respond to the direction of all those who are interested in using it, in helping it come to maturity.

The way the knuckles were born is perhaps a strange story, and certainly an exciting one. The little details often lead us onto an unknown path.

The secret to any discovery can be found in one trait — curiosity. Curiosity has made people bump into the most unexpected things; following the thread of the unexpected has often led to the development of a new product.

Ivory,® "the soap that floats," was the result of a technician's error at Proctor and Gamble. Something quite salvageable and enduring came out of that unexpected moment. More laboratory accidents than we might imagine have created many items we take for granted today. Those accidents happened in the course of ordinary, everyday business. Someone, doing what was expected, let down his guard for a moment, and with one altered detail, met the unexpected.

DISCOVERY

Here are the ingredients that went into the knuckles' discovery and development.

1. A CLIENT, who had consulted with me some months before, back for another session.

2. A REQUEST, as usual, that she put her hands down on the table so I could check the position of her hands, the spaces between the fingers, and the appearance of her nails.

3. A GLANCE that revealed a deep line on the tip knuckle of one of her fingers, that had not been there during her last visit.

4. A REALIZATION that when a line appears on the palm or changes in any way, there is a meaning attached to it.

5. A QUESTION in my mind, that if the lines' changes on the palm are significant, why wouldn't this change also mean something on the back of the hands?

6. A STRONG DESIRE to get a better look at the new line, as if a closer view of it just might reveal the mystery of its appearance on the tip knuckle.

At this point, I asked to pick up her hand, and I lifted the tip knuckle up to get a clearer look at it.

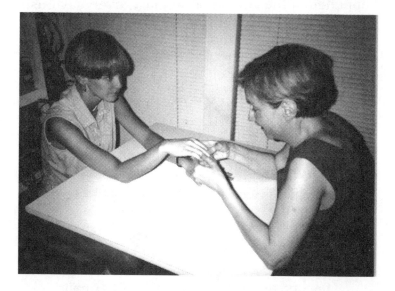

As I brought her hand closer to my line of vision, I was dumbstruck. I was not seeing that new tip line at all, but another thing entirely … a whole world of images, a series of tiny lines in recognizable patterns, on her middle knuckle. The patterns were made up of tiny stick figures, such as a child would draw. They looked like warriors.

The shock of that image and the realization that after eighteen years of a routine look at the back of the hands, I was seeing something that had undoubtedly always been there, unnoticed, made quite an impact. A sense of disbelief took over, as well as a very real determination to make something of the discovery, to come to grips with the meaning of such an incredible situation.

The moment of excited exclamations passed quickly, and the client and I returned to our regular session. Although my mind was on the routine in front of me, I knew this day was a passage to uncharted territory.

I already knew and loved the hands well. I never imagined, in my wildest dreams, that a whole new world of interpretation lay untouched, on the surface of something I looked at every day.

Nor did I think of it then in those terms. I only knew I would begin to look at every knuckle on every set of hands that came across my table, and I would not stop until I could account for the scenes that met my eye on each knuckle.

The material was there. What to do with it? In many ways, the answer was to proceed as always, not disrupting the sessions my clients had come to expect, but adding a little extra to each one. No client objected to that. They more they could hear and experience, the better, as far as they were concerned.

THE IMPORTANCE OF QUESTIONS

My clients were used to my approach: ask questions and more questions. My original motivation for that style was a desire to put people at ease, to give them a chance to relax and have a sense of participation in their own reading.

A look at *Palmistry: The Whole View,* page 13, will show a concern for this issue. The reader is warned, "Do you enjoy genuine dialogue with the other person, and are you prepared to receive as much input from him as possible?"

I never knew just how much could be gained from such an approach, years later, in the development of the knuckle material. I only knew that people must be comfortable with the process of consultation, if the session is to be a success. And that a palmist must not appear to play God, or to speak in absolutes. The way around that was to ask questions.

When people are asked if something is true about them, that the hands reveal, they are given a chance to validate themselves, to confirm or deny the information. This process alone gives them some control and lets them learn something in the moment to take home and think about, not swallow whole. Only with intelligent reflection can a person benefit from a hand reading session; never more so than if the session has made the client think while sitting at the table.

Asking questions about the information in the palm also gave me an opportunity to learn things I could learn no other way — from direct experience, and straight from the living article, the client.

In the process of discovering what type of information the knuckles could reveal, nothing was more important than the urge and ability to ask questions. The intensity and type of questions increased. In the original work with the knuckles, there was not a sense of straightforward discussion as there had been with the palm.

With the palm I knew exactly what I was aiming for; the books had taught me what everything meant. I did want to confirm what was already given. With the knuckles, I had only a small idea of what I was aiming for, truly a shot in the dark, as I began. So my questions became wide-ranging and all-inclusive, a stab at any possible meaning.

STARTING TO ORGANIZE

How was I going to unravel this mystery? Where to start with the intriguing discovery of images in the knuckles? How to organize the material?

Two significant starting points came from premises in palmistry, and surprisingly, handwriting analysis.

First, standard palmistry has meanings for each finger. I modified these meanings slightly, and let each finger define, by its meaning, the significance of any figure found in the knuckles. As an example, the index finger has always been associated with leadership and public image. In the new system, the index finger became the career finger. Any information found in the knuckles of either index finger would then be expected to relate to career and work.

Second, those wonderful stick figures, the warriors, that I first saw in knuckles were not uniformly drawn. Each figure had limbs of different length and depth. The right arm on one figure could be short, the left arm long. One of the legs could be etched more deeply than the other, giving one a firm appearance and the other a faint appearance.

In handwriting analysis, the length and depth of strokes makes a difference in the interpretation of each letter. Just knowing that gave me a clue that I might apply these distinctions to the figures. As expected, a deeper line would have more meaning than a faint one. A deep line, whether it was an arm or leg, would emphasize that limb over the other one.

IDENTIFYING THE DIRECTION OF EACH LIMB

Now, how would I apply the key of different depth and length on the limbs of the figures? Here again, an experimental approach worked beyond expectation. A matter of inspiration took over. As it happened, while I worked with a client, the client's seat at the table was in the north, and because I sat directly across from the client, I sat in the south. Remember, the figures in the knuckles faced me, as the client would extend a hand.

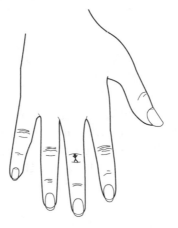

The head automatically became the north part of the figure, the legs the south, and the arms fell into the east and west directions.

VARIATIONS IN WARRIORS' APPEARANCE

A variation on the warriors' figures was soon found. Many warriors appeared to be carrying weapons — a club, a stick, a sword, or a shield. These details only added to the clear impression of a warrior going into battle.

A year or so after the discovery of warriors in the knuckles, a copy of them was found, purely by accident, in a book. These figures in the book were a representation of the script for the Indus Valley Civilization, a culture contemporary with that of ancient Egypt.

One more baffling detail surfaced. The same figures were also found on wooden tablets in the Easter Islands, half a world away. These figures, drawn in identical postures to the Indus Valley figures, were rendered more fully, with a double set of lines.

These scripts have not been deciphered, but it is tempting to think that a basic clue to their meaning lies in their posture.

FULLY DRAWN FIGURES

A second set of figures appeared in the knuckles. These little figures looked like cartoon drawings, with circular heads, inflated bodies, and puffy limbs. Hands and feet were not drawn in detail, but just like a cartoon character.

Men, women, children, and animals all appeared in this type of image. The human figures might have hair corresponding to a typical male, female, or child's hairstyle. Or they might have no hair, just a circle for a head.

Two things distinguished these figures: the direction they faced in the knuckles, or their profile; and their dress. Each figure faces to the front, the side, or the back. Each figure has full dress details. The women wear skirts, blouses, dresses, and gowns. Men wear slacks and a shirt, suits, overcoats, and even a tuxedo or formal wear. Children, depending on age, appear in diapers or play clothes, particularly overalls and casual outfits. Infants often appear wrapped in blankets, with just a circle for the head visible.

It was clear that the interpretation of these figures would be different from that of the warriors, because the figures were not dynamic like the warriors, leaping about or pointing vigorously in one direction. The figures seemed to be a "still life" version of reality. Because their dress and profile emerged as their particular "handles," these were the obvious features to interpret.

IDENTIFICATION

The process of identifying the figures began with the warriors, because they were discovered first.

Now, imagine a figure appearing on the index knuckle. The left arm of the figure is longer. The figure faces out, and the image is the reverse of the person looking at it. If you are looking at a figure on the knuckles, your right arm lines up with the figure's left arm. See that the left arm faces east. This will always be true of the left arm of a figure. That arm is in the east sector, and the right arm of the warrior figure is in the west. The image is on the work finger knuckle.

I began my research with an obvious question: "Do you, or your boss, or anyone important at your job, have any business in the east?" since the figure clearly emphasized something about the east with that long arm.

The client said, "Yes, my boss goes to New York on business every month." Then to clarify whether the figure could refer to anyone else besides the boss, I asked, "Does anyone else besides the boss work in the east?" The client said no. It was obvious that the figure in the knuckle represented the boss.

This was the first step: establishing the identity of the figure in the knuckle.

POSTURE

Through the client's response, I knew the figure in her index finger knuckle had to be her boss, since he was the one who went east for business.

Now that I had that detail secured, what to do with it? The point was to give the client some information, to interpret the tale of the figure.

This figure was not a simple line, such as a life line or a head line, but it had the same characteristics offered for analysis — length, depth, and direction of lines. Rather than applying to a single line, length was used to describe each of the limbs; rather than describing a whole line, depth was used to define one or two limbs on the figure; and rather than considering direction as coming from one mount and going to another, as lines in the palm are analyzed, direction for the figures in the knuckles became literal.

To contrast the figures again with the lines of the palm, one critical difference remained. Lines on the palm lacked a quality the figures had — posture! Because each figure was a representation of a human being, the new ingredient for analysis, and a very obvious one, was the figure's posture.

Some of the warriors stood tall, some had arms raised in apparent victory; others looked stooped, with sagging shoulders and limp arms.

To continue the analysis, once I established the identity of a figure in a knuckle, the next step was to use the posture of the figure to describe the person's state of mind or emotions, and to predict a future for the present image.

FURTHER DETAILS

This warrior boss, found on my client's index knuckle, had a positive posture, a dynamic pose, with arms lifted upward. The client confirmed that her boss was an upbeat type, never knew defeat, and was quite successful in his work. I used her confirmation and the warrior's posture to predict success for him on his next trip to New York.

And that was how it all began. To conclude the story, how was I to know whether the prediction for the boss turned out? From the client's report later, once the event happened.

Year after year of working with people, recording information, and accumulating the results produced the system recorded here today.

There really was more to tell. How could I put the predictions in a time frame? When would that boss have that successful trip to New York?

Let's look at timing, how it works in the palm, and contrast that approach with timing in the knuckles.

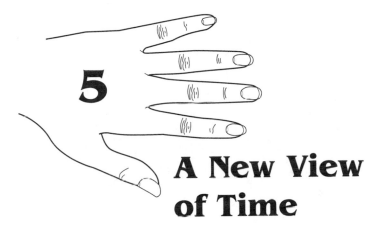

5

A New View of Time

According to the current system for telling time in the hand, we use the life line and the fate line as the main index of time. And in our wisdom we have set the palm up to represent a possible eighty-year life span. We had to set a boundary, an endpoint, to be able to mark off the intervening years. But nowhere is it stated that a person can't live more than eighty years. For people older than eighty, we can simply assume that they have not come to the end of their life line — yet! In this case, we adjust our input according to other signs in the hand. We are not trying, in any case, to predict the length of a person's life when we time matters in the hand.

A word here about that very issue. Since modern palmistry does not predict the length of life, it is okay to look at the hands of anyone and say, "I'm sorry, I just don't have a clue how long you're going to live!"

People have always wanted to believe that hands can predict the length of life, and maybe, in

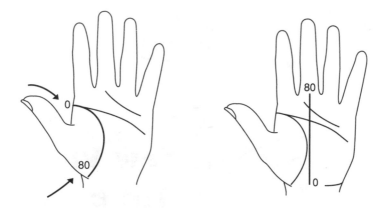

Time diagrammed on the life and fate lines

earlier eras of history, like the ones we reviewed in the introduction to this book, when there were fewer variables to life, it was possible to predict the length of life from a hand.

Today we don't do that in the more accepted forms of palmistry passed down in books. The very idea of predicting the length of a life at all bears a little thought. Do you know anyone who can do that? A good way to look at it is that your religious leaders cannot predict how long you will live, your doctor cannot, and Einstein himself could not do it. Why would a palmist, who has only seen your hand, be able to tell you how long you are going to live, when no one else in this scientific age can?

Many times vulnerable palmists, eager to please, will allow the pressure of peoples' insistent attitudes to sway them into making a stab at the matter, especially in a party setting.

That is all right, if it's done in the spirit of a "guess," with the explanation that we can't really see any such thing in the hand today. A disclaimer is necessary because the information is not truly available from today's system, and any date given can make a person uncomfortable, or become a point of unhealthy fixation. Palmists are here to make life a little better for their clients and friends, not to be the cause of an obsession.

Apart from not predicting length of life from the palm, the life line helps us pinpoint established years in a person's life.

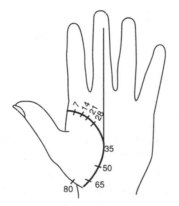

We divide the life line in half by drawing a line down the middle of the middle finger, and extending it until it intersects the life line. This mark is thirty-five years of age. The time before thirty-five is marked off in five sets of seven years each.

Because the life line is set up to represent eighty years — a lot of time in one small space — we cannot break time down into any smaller segments on this line. After looking at the diagram, you can see it is quite a feat just to manage those divisions. With practice, you can become quite accurate at predicting time using this system.

The life line is only the first indicator of time on the palm. After this line, we look at the fate line. It has its own eighty-year span.

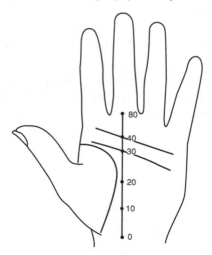

The most important years on the fate line are the first thirty, the time a person uses to set up a life, put a career into motion, and establish a family. The first thirty years are traced from the wrist to the head line. The thirties themselves are all enclosed in the space between the head and heart lines. At the heart line, the fate line reaches forty — a big intersection in anybody's life, as well as in their hand!

Notice how the remaining forty years are "jam-packed" into the remaining part of the palm, from the heart line up to the top of the palm. This small space is divided into four sections of ten years each, coming up to the total of eighty.

Working with time from the age of forty onward in the hands, on the fate line, can be a bit tricky, as the space is small; and, because, after forty, people are more likely to begin doing something more in line with their heart's desire, especially during their retirement years. Time and emotion do funny things together. Time flies when a person is involved with a cherished project or loved one. Time, as it appears in the palm, works the same way. It "flies" by in the small space allotted to the years forty through eighty.

Occasionally palmists will time the head and heart lines. However, these lines are a secondary source, not a primary one, for telling time in the hands.

Viewing time in one-year increments has always been useful and still works for many of our needs today. However, the new system gives us additional windows on time, shortening the traditional view from one year at a time, to increments of months, weeks, and days.

A QUICKER WAY TO TELL TIME

The back of the hand turns out to be a mini-cosmos of the palm. The tiniest of spaces, the knuckles, take their turn as the main conveyors of information. If you think the palm is a small area to work from, get used to the idea of a spot about 1/10th the size of the palm. It would be hard to imagine that a world exists in the knuckles, and we are about to set out on our exploration of this very world with this first technique, a way to advance time and condense it into smaller increments.

The world of the knuckles is tinier, more condensed, and packed with infinitely more information than a first glance would warrant. In this new system, we are just beginning to appreciate all that a smaller area of the hands has to offer, as a specialty related directly to standard palmistry.

In palmistry, people are most concerned with timing events. So it is appropriate to understand first how time can be diagrammed in the knuckles. In Chapter 6, we will have a deeper look at this method. For now, we must understand that time on the knuckles is divided into two different tracks, because each hand has a different function.

TWO WORLDS OF THE HAND

We have already seen that there are two worlds of palmistry applied to the hand as a whole. The palm side of the hand represents our personal world, a world in which we have some control and make decisions; the back side of the hand represents the "real world," and events and people over whom we have less control.

In this new system, there is a difference, too, between the left hand and the right hand, when we look at time. In ordinary palmistry, the dominant hand has a different role than the nondominant hand. Emphasis is given to the material on the dominant hand, while the information from the other hand must be incorporated to create a balanced picture of a person's potential.

The same thing is true with the back of the hands; the information from both hands must be taken into consideration to get an accurate picture. And, just as we have always had an organized system for analyzing information from the palms, we will have a sequence to follow as we look at the knuckles.

In the original palmistry, the dominant hand is the right hand for a right-handed person, and the left hand for a left-handed person. This is also the case in the new system. Whichever hand a person uses is the dominant hand.

NAMES FOR THE HANDS AND SEQUENCE OF USE

To make our work easier in this system, we are going to rename the hands. We look at the nondominant hand first, because this hand has background information which will orient us to the "big picture" of a person's world. Then we look at the dominant hand to bring the picture of a person's world into sharper focus and to define the most immediate issues that need attention.

Because we will look at the nondominant hand first, we will name it the "first hand." The dominant hand will be called the "second hand." This designation does not signify greater or lesser importance, but only the sequence in which the hands will be used to interpret all that the knuckles have to offer.

FOUR SETS OF KNUCKLES

There are four sets of knuckles to be analyzed, in total, from the back of the hands. We are going to work with the knuckles that are most closely connected with the fingers' movement, the middle and tip knuckles. The knuckles which join the fingers to the hands are not involved in our technique.

In this system, we have two sets of knuckles on the first hand to analyze, and two on the second hand.

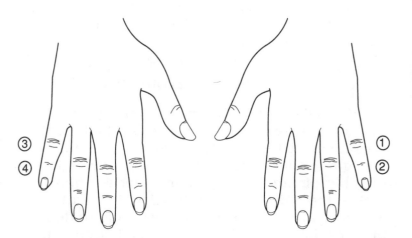

On the second hand:
Set 3: middle knuckles
Set 4: tip knuckles

On the first hand:
Set 1: middle knuckles
Set 2: tip knuckles

Time on the First Hand

On the first hand, we will find information about the past and the future. We find both types of time here because this hand reflects past that will affect the future, and a preview of that future. For both sets of knuckles, the future will cover a possible three-year period of time, from today forward. On the first set of knuckles, the past will go back to a year or more ago; on the second set of knuckles, to six months ago.

On the first hand:

Set 1: the middle knuckles
Past: One or more years ago.
Future: Today and up to three years ahead.

Set 2: the tip knuckles
Past: Six months ago.
Future: Up to three years ahead in time.

Time on the Second Hand

On the second hand, the dominant hand, we are looking at the present and the future. The third set of knuckles relates to the present, while the tip knuckles speak of the future, from six to eighteen months ahead. Time then on this hand ranges from the present to eighteen months ahead.

On the second hand:

Set 3: the middle knuckles
The present.

Set 4: the tip knuckles
From six months ahead at the main crease, up to eighteen months ahead at the tip of the fingers.

This view is only an introduction to time on the knuckles. A more detailed approach will be covered in Chapter 6. For now, just to know that we can see time in segments of up to three years ahead on the first hand, and up to eighteen months ahead on the second hand, is enough.

Timing of the Palm's Information

In a sense, time has accelerated in the palm as well as on the back of the hand. Although our timing system here talks in terms of years, we do have ways to know how important any one piece of information on a palm is, on a more immediate basis.

The importance of a piece of information makes it stand out, literally, on the palm, and asks for our attention now.

When we consider that a palm has eighty years of potential information to decipher, it's nice to know that we can focus on exactly what matters, discarding any peripheral information.

When we look at a palm, we are immediately confronted with a tangle of lines. It is our job to sort them out. Older palmistry has always allowed for this need by defining the major and minor lines, and each of their tasks. We know exactly what the life line, and all the other lines, stands for. But what exactly is the story we are going to extract from the palm? And how are we going to touch on what matters most? Are we going to tell a tale that begins in our corner and stretches to China, or are we going to stick to a subject? How can we?

Easily. We already know that the main lines must tell us something important. We know that any other deep and well-defined lines also want to speak. But which lines speak first? What is the protocol? A new clue will let you know.

A SHINE ON THE PALM

Look carefully and you will see first that the surface of the palm, at least in some areas, has a shine. Get used to that. Then look again and notice that some of the lines, whether they are large or small, deep or thin, also have a shine. Where the shine occurs on a line, this is equivalent to using a yellow highlighter, as students do, to mark material they are reading and want to recall. The shine on the lines says, "Notice me!"

Little bits of the story to be translated from the palm now come from the lines that look the most "alive," with a shine and perhaps a heightened color, usually pink, surrounding them.

The shine and the heightened color mean the line is "activated;" that its story is active now. The shiny and pink sections on the lines, anywhere they occur in the hand, are used to predict the future. These clues are a way to select what is important to tell, out of all the information a palm might give, and to predict an outcome precisely because the present — highlighted for your convenience! — is accounted for. The present is the support in the hand on which spins the future.

THE IMPORTANCE OF THE PRESENT TIME

"No time like the present" — you remember that saying. Nowhere is its meaning more apropos than in its application to the palm and the knuckles, and to their ability to reveal time in the hand.

How do you figure the hand can even begin to be a vehicle to project the future? Most certainly the hand could not give us future dates if a strong picture of the present did not come first. The future does not operate in a vacuum, either in the hands or in life.

Think about this: We all have much more of a "past" than we can use in any one moment or in any one situation. There are also multiple possible futures for each of us. We could theoretically choose to do anything — to marry, to divorce, to get a new job, to get five more degrees. But what will we actually do? The life we lead in the present is the most natural step to our future. Our lives are organic, evolving from one moment to the next.

Perhaps as a child you took a magnifying glass and caught the sun's rays, concentrating them in a bright circle through the action of the glass. The rays burned fiercely in their concentrated spot.

The heat of the concentrated rays, from the tiny focus created by the glass, took on a life of its own. This is exactly what the focus of the present does for our lives. The action takes on a heat of its own and produces the effect we call our future.

A Small Story

Every action we take has a past and a future attached to it. A small story might make this clearer. Let's say you and your mate have just celebrated your first wedding anniversary. You are very happy and the year has gone well.

You sit back to think about the past, to reminisce and appreciate how far you have come down the path you have chosen together. You recall the day you met, and exclaim how glad you are that you each decided to take that cruise. He almost had to cancel his plans when his boss wanted to plan an unexpected trip to the coast to supervise the installation of a new project. And you thought maybe a trip to Paris, among all those exciting French men, might be better. But then the thought of the water, of five days of relaxation under the sun and perfect skies, won out. Then his boss decided to wait another week for his project.

The critical part of the past which brought you together is the simple fact that you ended up on the same boat at the same time. What his boss was planning at that time, a possible meeting, will in no way affect your future now. What you were thinking, how fun it would be to meet a few romantic French men, no longer has any appeal or part in your plans.

As you talk, the phone suddenly rings. Friends you are planning to spend the weekend with, to further celebrate your anniversary, are calling to confirm your plans and announce that they got tickets to that concert everyone said was sold out.

You are excited to hear about the tickets, but as you resume your conversation, just the two of you, you dwell on the fact that your life together is rapidly preparing you for further plans. Your dream is to go to New Zealand for a two-month hiking trip. You have saved nearly enough money, and are each working to get enough time off for this trip. And you are doing this precisely at this time because, when you have had your adventure, you think it will then be time to think about having a baby.

The phone call a moment ago made only a few ripples on your consciousness, yet it fits in the picture of the moment. The occasion you are celebrating, your anniversary and the foundation you have built in your marriage, will be in focus this weekend. After the weekend, you will be right back at work, working toward your dream trip.

Sorting Out the Story

Here's how we would locate your story and its time frame in the knuckles. The first set of knuckles refers to events at least a year old. Here we would find a record of your wedding, and prior to that, the events leading up to it. We would find a record of your meeting, since your meeting a year and a half ago led to the wedding a year ago.

We would not find much record of either his boss' plans or your thoughts before the cruise, as they will not affect your future.

Meeting each other did and will continue to affect the future, so the meeting can appear in the knuckles. The wedding, although already in the past, is your ticket to the future.

The second set of knuckles will talk about the progress you have made in the last six months. Featured on these knuckles will be indications of travel in the future, along with signs of hard work and financial planning in the last six months that will make the trip possible.

The third set of knuckles will reveal your contentment in the present, and the continued focus on your desire for your trip. The celebration for the upcoming weekend might show up as part of the present, made possible by the very fact you are married; or the celebration might not show up in these knuckles because it will not be a significant part of your future. The determining factor in what shows up is the focus of events, and the brain carefully selects most effectively the images that portray the story and the nature of the reality that surrounds you.

On the fourth set of knuckles, we will find the prediction of your trip. Even though you are not sure yet just which month you will be able to leave, your unconscious mind knows this date, and relays it through the symbolism on the knuckles.

The knuckles take the central, most important fact, your marriage, and reveal what significantly led up to it (the past) and what will follow (the future). The hiking trip shows up because your first hand shows events for up to three years ahead in time; any one of the eight knuckles on that hand could carry hints about the baby, as well as information about your meeting, the cruise, and your wedding, because having a baby is a natural outcome of that central fact.

And if, by any chance, you were going to conceive that baby, say, on your trip to New Zealand, clues about the baby would be launched in the knuckles at the same time as the trip. More indications of a baby would show up on the fourth set of knuckles.

Perhaps this story has helped you grasp how the knuckles carry the information they do. A central, important fact is shown in context, in its past and its future projections. All relevant past and future attached to any event gets painted in the knuckles' picture.

There is no present without a past, and no present without a future, as far as the knuckles are concerned.

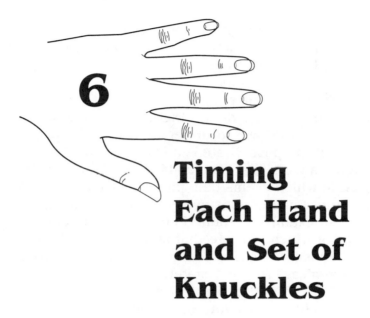

6

Timing
Each Hand
and Set of
Knuckles

Time is a very interesting issue, and a more complicated one than we might imagine. Ordinarily we don't have to give any thought to how we view time, we simply experience it.

But, for certain purposes, we have to look at how time operates and how we have structured it to express reality. Understanding languages is a case in point. Different people through their languages have different concepts of reality, and therefore, different verb forms to depict the concept of action.

Palmistry, in its symbolic interpretation of reality, is a language, too; a language which tells a story with reference to a past, present, and a future.

To tell a good story from the hands, we must keep our facts in order, and that means concentrating first on the past, not on the future — the gravy everyone wants to hear about!

To look at the past in the hands, when we are using the back side of the hand, fingers, and knuckles, we have to understand that the past is not just the past. There is a simple past where an event happens just once and is over. And there is a past in which events take place over and over. We use these expressions every day in our speech.

An example is found in these two statements, both of which indicate that something took place in the past: "I went to Jamaica," and "I used to go to Jamaica." The first statement implies that you went once in the past. The second statement appears to say that you went more than once.

There are better examples yet of these two types of past time. Think about a marriage, a university degree, or a career that is built over a period of years. These realities are not over in an instant or even a day. The past they contain reflects an enduring reality.

Now imagine getting a phone call from a friend overseas, from the far ends of the earth. A surprise, and an event not likely to happen again soon. Or getting a windfall check in the mail, another event which is not likely to repeat itself anytime soon.

When we look at the knuckles, our first task is to understand the nature of the person's "repeat" or enduring reality, and what bearing those experiences over a long period of time have on the possible future ahead. This is done by checking the information in the nondominant hand.

Our second job is to look at the action of the moment, and to judge the likely outcome of present circumstances and events.

When we look to the future, as a culture, we are very bottom line-oriented. We gear ourselves to look for events. We narrow our focus. For this reason, a person is more likely to ask a palmist, "Am I going to get a divorce?" than "Tell me about the ongoing ups and downs in my marriage." The process, when the person looks to the future, is not of much interest; the outcome is.

This is what the tip knuckles of the dominant hand give us — the short-term outcome of present circumstances and events.

THE DIFFERENT TIME ROLES OF THE TWO HANDS

Let's look at the different roles of the two hands, then. The first hand, the nondominant hand, always gives the background for any situation, no matter which finger it is taken from: career on the index, money on the middle, relationships on the ring, and negotiations on the little finger.

The first hand has a wider focus, showing the ongoing reality of any particular situation.

The second hand automatically moves to a tighter focus in its story, because it will first reveal the details of the present, through the signs of the middle knuckles. In this system, the present is a four-month span of time. Obviously, not nearly so much can go on in four months, in any story, as can happen in years and decades. That is why the focus is tighter.

Because the future, which is revealed by the tip of the knuckles of the second hand, is event-oriented, the focus stays tight for these knuckles, too.

We could say that the first hand has a long-term reality attached to it, while the second hand has a short-term reality. Think of the information in the first hand as the "big picture" and the information in the second hand as the "nitty-gritty." Using the information of both hands in a set order, we can understand the background of any situation, its present development, and its future outcome.

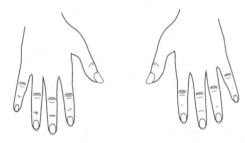

Nitty-gritty　　　　　　　　*Big picture*

PAST TIME FRAME FOR EACH HAND

How does the past show up in the two hands? What are the specifics? Most of our past shows up in the first hand. Only the two months just past show up in the middle knuckles of the second hand.

The first set of knuckles has the capability of showing a large past. Their focus is the widest of all. The past they show ranges anywhere from just one year ago, to all the way back to birth.

Past

Nondominant hand: set 1

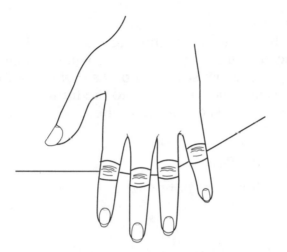

All four middle knuckles range in time past from one year ago back to birth. Because this set of knuckles must give the relevant details from the past that will affect the future, these knuckles present the important details, whether they occurred at birth, age nine, or last year! Start your work with knuckles and the questions by assuming the information is only a year old.

Only dialogue with the client about what you are seeing will help establish the exact year of any situation you do find in these knuckles. Your guideline as you do your job is the knowledge that the information from the first set of knuckles is bound to be at least one year old. You can begin to work from that point.

Ask your client, "Did such-and-such happen a year ago?" Then take your clue from the client's answer. The event may be two years old, not one. Only your client can tell you exactly when an event portrayed in the middle knuckles of the first hand happened. Your job is to find the event as part of a past that matters to the future.

When you get to the second set of knuckles on the first hand, you find out what's been happening in the last several months that will lead into the present, and from there to the future. A view of an average of six months in the past shows up in these knuckles.

Immediate Past

Nondominant hand: set 2

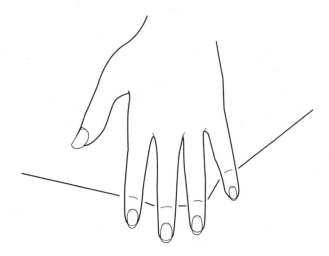

All four tip knuckles range in time from six months in the past.

The focus of the amount of the past we can see in the dominant hand rapidly narrows. All the past we have to account for on this hand is found in the third set of knuckles, the present knuckles. A span of four months is allotted to these knuckles.

Of these four months, two are assigned to the past, designed to be a lead-in to the actual moment, and refer to the past eight weeks. The remaining two months to be decoded on the present knuckles cover an eight-week period of time in the future.

Two Months Ago

Dominant hand: set 3

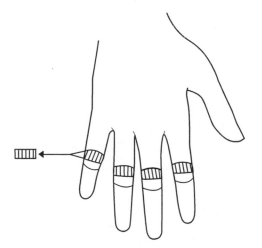

The back section of the middle knuckles, the shaded section in the diagram, represents eight weeks ago. The blank section represents the second half of the middle knuckles and its time frame of eight weeks ahead.

THE PRESENT TIME FRAME

To define the present, time is divided into the two segments we see above, one of eight weeks past, and the other of eight weeks ahead. This is due to the fact that whatever is occurring in the present has to have a lead-in, a short period of time to pave the way. And in the greater scheme of things, in light of a lifetime, eight weeks ago is practically the present.

The same rationale holds for designating eight weeks in the future as the present. That eight weeks, in the span of a lifetime, is really the now. And, yes, there is a way to see "today" in the present knuckles. There is a today line.

Today

Dominant hand: set 3

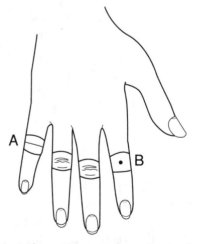

The center line (A) represents today. If there is no line in the exact center of the knuckle, make the center (B) of the knuckle today. Occasionally the line is a little off-center. That's okay; the line is used anyway.

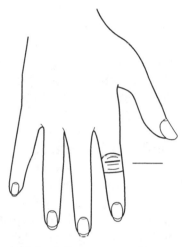

The space behind the center line, representing eight weeks ago, is smaller than the space on the other side of the line, which represents eight or more weeks ahead. Time at the very bottom of this knuckle is extended, because the second half of the knuckle is larger.

On rare occasions, you won't find a line at the exact center of the knuckle or off-center, either. In that case, go ahead and use the center of the knuckle as a marker for today, as if the line were there. Make the center a point of reference, not a hard and fast line, since knuckles do vary in their lines and ridges. Like snowflakes, knuckles are not all strictly alike.

FUTURE TIME FRAME FOR EACH HAND

Considering the past and how it is divided on the back of the hand is our first clue that each hand, as it portrays time, has a different role. This distinction is true for the future, too.

Because the first hand shows a longer period of the past, it has a longer projection into the future than the second hand. The future in the non-dominant, or first hand, ranges from one day to three years ahead. The future scene in the dominant, or second hand, projects only eighteen months ahead.

Predictions made from either set of knuckles on the first hand can come true within a day. But this rarely happens, and the average amount of time a prediction takes to work out from the first hand is two to three years, research has shown. After three years, the "statute of limitations" seems to run out, as if there were an expiration date for the reality to emerge from a certain set of possibilities. If a prediction made has not come true within three years, you can scrap it, and realize that not every potential comes to full flower.

The same is true if a prediction made for a period of six to eighteen months ahead does not occur within the outer limit of a year and a half.

Only a waiting game, and feedback from clients and friends, will let you know how long each prediction took to materialize. It is amazing how much does emerge. It is wonderful to think that our brains know our future with precision, in certain cases, that far ahead!

Future

Nondominant hand: both sets

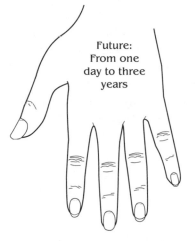

Future:
From one
day to three
years

The future time frame for both sets of knuckles is from one day up to three years ahead.

The future range on the second, or dominant, hand is different. The focus becomes tighter, as we have seen. The present knuckle singles out specific issues that capture our attention in the moment. The future knuckles, the tip knuckles, reveal the outcome of those issues.

Because we are aware of our issues in the present moment, we are able to use deliberate control to make conscious choices. This extra degree of focus, or control, narrows the time range for the working out of present issues.

The maximum range of prediction on the dominant hand is up to eighteen months in the future. Along the way, we find markers for the weeks and months ahead.

DIVIDING THE PRESENT KNUCKLE INTO WEEKS

On the present knuckle, it is possible to see time in terms of weeks. This knuckle has a greater number of ridges which allow us to divide time into smaller segments. When we get to the tip knuckles, we will talk in terms of months in the future.

To see time in terms of weeks, move forward from the today line or mark in the middle knuckle, dividing the ridges as shown on the following page.

Future

Dominant hand: set 3

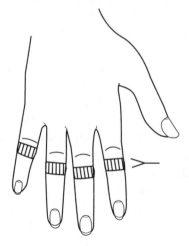

The space from the today line to the bottom edge of the knuckle represents the whole eight weeks.

The easiest way to begin to separate the space from the center line to the end of the knuckle into weeks is first to divide the space in half. Halfway across the space, we come to the one-month mark; at the end of the knuckle, we reach the two-month mark.

Four Weeks and Eight Weeks in the Future

Dominant hand: set 3

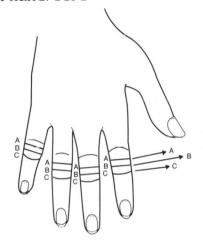

A—Today line
B—4 weeks ahead
C—8 weeks ahead

The division can be applied to all of the knuckles, as you can see in the diagram.

Point A to point B represents the first four weeks. Point B to point C represents the next four weeks.

So, you can move from A to B, or one-half of the knuckle's surface, to see how weeks one through four away from the present will be. Move from point B to point C, the remaining half of the knuckle, to determine what is happening in weeks five through eight away from the present.

You can judge time either in terms of two months away from the present or in terms of eight weeks. To visualize the weeks separately, divide

Today

8 Weeks
Ahead

each four-week section into four parts. That will give you a reference point for one week at a time.

One-fourth of space A to B is one week. One-half of space A to B represents two weeks. Three-fourths of space A to B covers a span of three weeks. The whole space is one month, or four weeks.

The small lines in the diagram at left are today, and weeks two through eight ahead.

Six Months in the Future

When we reach the tip knuckle and its main line, the deepest horizontal line stretching across the knuckle, we are six months ahead in the future.

If there is no single deep horizontal line on this knuckle, only a series of tiny, feathery lines, use the juncture where the joint bends as the six-month mark, as shown at right. Not all knuckles have the single deep line, as shown at left.

Most often, however, you will find a line which distinguishes itself, which you can call the six-month mark.

Five Months in the Future

Now, assume you find a tiny line just above the deep line, behind it, between the middle knuckle and the deep line itself. That tiny line, as shown to the right, is the five-month mark.

Four Months in the Future

Occasionally, there are two tiny lines behind the six-month mark; the one furthest back from the single deep line is the four-month mark. An example of this is shown below to the right.

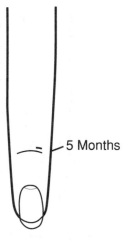

5 Months

We usually have a gap between the two-month mark at the end of the middle knuckle, and the next marker, whether it is a four-, five-, or six-month line you next encounter on the tip knuckle.

You might wonder where you can see the third month in the future. Often this month does not show. Sometimes the fourth and fifth months do not have a mark, either. You can assume that months three, four, and five are times when things are "in the hopper," and no outcome is visible yet. Just because there is no line to mark the exact track an event is on, does not mean something is not happening! This is rather like a pregnancy you cannot see, but which is actively developing, all hidden away.

4 Months
5 Months

Is there never a third month ahead available for viewing, might be your next question. Interestingly enough, there is a way to see the third month ahead. Did you really think one month would be arbitrarily left out altogether? It's just that this month is the least visible in the knuckle system, and you need to be advised that you might not see any indication of it in some hands.

This is how you would see it. Some middle knuckles are unevenly shaped, with the bottom half noticeably larger than the top half. Remember, the top half shows the past eight weeks; the bottom half, if the knuckle is evenly shaped, shows the next eight weeks ahead.

When the bottom half of the knuckle is larger, then the last ridge of the knuckle can be called the third month. This line is shown in the diagram at left.

Third Month in the Future

In the beginning, it is not necessary to be concerned about seeing a third month on the middle or present knuckle. It is enough to know that the whole knuckle contains a four-month period of time, with two months in the immediate past, and two in the immediate future. You can feel perfectly free, until you get used to working with the knuckles, to think only in terms of months. Don't try to do predictions for a week at a time until you are ready.

We are nearly through with the time track of the knuckles. Just one little bit to go, at this point. We are now dealing in months, not weeks. We have to learn how to get from the six-month mark up to the next mark, eighteen months.

To do this, we divide the area between the six-month mark and the cuticle, at the base of the nail, into ten little sections. Yes, this is the most delicate way to look at this space: dividing it into ten equal sections. This is how you will locate six

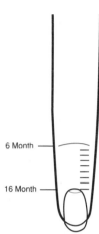

to sixteen months ahead in the future. These lines are shown on the diagram at right. The small lines represent months seven through fifteen. You will need to know the area — get acquainted with the territory, so to speak. But once you know the area allotted to this ten-month span of time, you will not need to read every bit of it. Not every part of the skin from the six-month line up to the cuticle will have lines or color on it to read.

There is a handy reference for looking a year ahead. The halfway point between the six- and sixteen-month marks is actually eleven months. This point is shown at right. But for the time when you are just getting used to this timing system, you can call that point one year in the future.

You can also easily find the seven-month line; it is the next small

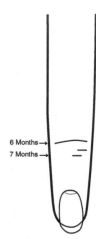

6 Months →
7 Months →

line after the six-month line. The line after that is the eight-month line. These are shown in the diagram to the left.

Where, at last, is the eighteen-month mark? The future time frame for the dominant hand, on the tip knuckles, is up to eighteen months ahead. So far we've just covered sixteen months on that knuckle.

The secret is, not all knuckles show information for the eighteen month time frame. But if they do, the way they do it is through lines or color that wrap around the side of the nail, close to the edge of the fingertip. (See the diagram below.)

Any line, symbol, mark, or color which appears along the side of the nail, in the flesh, from the cuticle down toward the manicured part of the nail, reveals something for eighteen months ahead. This area might contain lines as a continuation of an image that has started at the cuticle area, and signals that the conditions predicted for sixteen months in the future will continue to show up at eighteen months, as well.

This timing system is entirely new, and will take some getting used to. Work with it in stages. Look at the first set of knuckles to get a message about the past. Then try to get a piece of the puzzle, some information about events and conditions from the last six months, in the sec-

18 Months →

ond set of knuckles, that might produce a future situation. Check out the present in the middle knuckles of the dominant hand, and then, at last, look at the future knuckles to determine what will happen in six to eighteen months.

Here is a list which puts telling time from the knuckles in the simplest possible view.

Nondominant hand:

Middle: 1 year ago
Tip: 6 months ago
Both: 3 years ahead

Dominant hand:

Middle: now
Tip: 6 months ahead
Fingertips: 18 months ahead

You may have one further question, having looked at this introduction to the new timing system. Where did it all come from, and why can time be divided the way it is on the knuckles?

There is a simple answer to the first part of that question, and a more complicated one to the second.

The outline for this timing system came from a day-to-day working out of the knuckles' information, ten years of research, and constant verification of the role of time on the knuckles. The system developed as a matter of logic, through the experience of time as we know it, divided into past, present, and future.

PALM TIME VERSUS KNUCKLE TIME

But to answer why time is divided so neatly on the knuckles requires a look at time on the palm, and how signs in the palm manifest compared to the system in the knuckles.

Up front, we do have a timing system for the palm, which we have reviewed. There is no problem with assigning a time frame to the major lines. The thing is, those time frames apply equally to the major lines on the right and left hands. We do not divide time between the two palms as we do in the knuckles. Either palm contains the same time frame.

But there are two palms. Something seems left over, or superfluous, in contrast with every square inch of the knuckles assigned a different time frame. How do you deal with two palms? How do you synthesize the information and predict something accurately, if the system is not so well combined or straightforward as the knuckles' timing?

That challenge has been left to the individual palmist from time immemorial. The typical approach is to look at the most outstanding features on both palms, and mention them. Most of the time, the information is complementary, not contradictory.

But if the signs are contradictory, from one palm to another, the "winner" of the debate is always the dominant hand (the right hand for right-handed people, and the left hand for left-handed people), because that hand has more consciousness attached to it than the nondominant hand, which plays a supporting role.

It's interesting that people who do not know anything about palmistry pick up on the confusion between the two hands by asking, "Which hand was I born with?" That question always leaves the questioner wide open to a matter-of-fact answer — "Both!" But what the person is asking is whether all signs in one hand relate to given potential, and all signs in the other hand relate to how that potential is used.

The answer is no. Each palm contains information on given potential and how it is being used. Each day we use both hands to get through the day. It's fun to take that question about the use of the palms literally, and turn it back to the person, asking, "How many hands do you use to leave work, get in your car and drive home? Do you tie one hand behind your back so that only one of them can express the potential to get you home safely?"

A moment ago, we saw that the dominant hand is more conscious in its function than the other hand. Now let's look at how an impending event will manifest in both palms. In contrast to the knuckles, which have every stage of time marked off step by step, the outline of an event goes full circle in the palm.

Signs forecasting the event appear first in the nondominant hand, before the person involved is aware the event will happen. As soon as the person is aware of the event or the possibility it will happen, the signs move to the dominant hand. Once the event has happened and is forgotten, the signs move back to the nondominant hand.

Story

A little story will illustrate the way the two palms record reality. Let's pretend you have worked long and hard on a stage play, and want so much for it to be a success. You are not yet finished, though you've been working on it for three years.

You are not aware of this, but your left hand (you are right-handed) shows signs predicting fame and creative success. You keep on working, plugging away. Eventually, you think you've finally got it; the ending to your story is falling into place.

Next, you contact a producer. You didn't realize it, but little signs of fame have been creeping into your right hand. The producer is interested.

The signs of fame and creative success grow deeper in the right palm.

In another year, your play is on Broadway, and your right palm positively glows with signs of success. The play continues in its success for years, rivaling the run of Agatha Christie's *Mousetrap* in London.

By now, you are so used to the notion of your play being "out there," you have long since gone on to other things. You are farming turnips in Connecticut. You voraciously read every book on gardening you can find. You whistle your way through your gardens.

The signs of creative success and fame have receded in your right hand and have come back to roost in your left hand. There they remain, as a testimony of your ongoing success that you have gotten so used to, that you no longer give it a second thought. Work on the play and its production has ceased to grip your conscious awareness.

The left hand reflects a less conscious awareness, whether that includes an event that has happened or has yet to happen. But it cannot be said that that sign for creative success and fame, now in your left hand, means you never used that potential. Now the significance of that sign in your left hand is that it is a record of reality that surrounds you.

Time in the palm goes full circle. The influence of coming events, their reality, and later their memory flow from one hand to the other and back again.

On the fingers, time expresses itself more in sequence. From the further reaches of the past, to the recent past, to the immediate past, and on to the future — this straightforward march of time on the knuckles occurs because the fingers have a more conscious function than either palm.

How to look at this fact? By realizing that you can deliberately move your fingers. They are active, and conscious in their expression, if you choose to be conscious of them. Another word applies here. The use of your fingers, whether totally conscious or not in the moment, is *deliberate.* On top of that, you purposefully, consciously, direct your fingers.

You cannot change a thing about your palm deliberately and consciously. You can move your fingers on purpose. The motor function of the fingers comes from another part of the brain. The movement is more specialized and more conscious.

Specialization and consciousness give us time as we know it every day. Consciousness and the degree to which it governs the changes in the palms and fingers is the key to the different system of time we apply to the knuckles.

And, even with this explanation, we have failed to address the bottom line about time. That is that time, in the end, is a mystery. And no more motivated students of time can be found than palmists — except, perhaps, modern physicists!

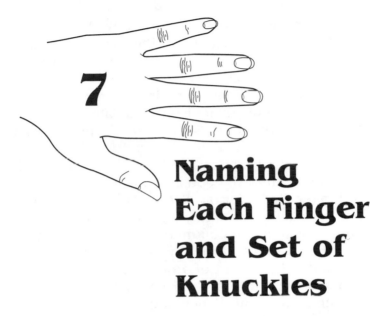

7

Naming Each Finger and Set of Knuckles

Never underestimate the importance of a name. How far would advertisers and bankers get without a name to lean on? How far would the postal service get in its deliveries if no one had a name?

The real power of names lies in the way they make the definition of reality possible. Names are an organizing principle in action. Products and people conform to their names, coming alive according to what they are called.

The fingers and knuckles are no exception. If we are to understand the nature of what they have to tell us, we have to know their names.

Occasionally, parents will wait days to observe their newborn before naming the infant, to see what name most wants to "stick." The fingers and knuckles have also been named with this system. After a period of observation, the following names emerged as the best markers of the reality of the fingers and knuckles.

In modern palmistry, the index finger is called Jupiter, the middle finger is named Saturn, the ring finger is known as Apollo, and the little finger as Mercury.

These names reflect the type of energy associated with each of the gods: expansion and power for Jupiter; limits for old Father Time, Saturn; the joy of creativity for sunny Apollo; the rewards of communication and commerce for wily Mercury.

When we look at the fingers from the back of the hand only, as part of a new view of palmistry, we adapt the name to the role each finger plays. The function of the finger does not substantially change when the back of the hand is the focus, and the names for the fingers from the back are only modifications of the original names.

Jupiter, the index finger, has always stood for leadership, and the capacity to make one's presence felt and to make a difference in the world. To establish its role on the back of the hand, the best way to summarize its significance is to call it the career finger. Through our careers, we can indeed make a difference in the world and make our presence felt. A career is just the vehicle for that very purpose.

Saturn, the middle and longest finger, has always been considered the "balance wheel" of the hand, the measure of a person's conscience and sense of duty. Knowing the details of a Saturn finger gives insight into a person's values. What matters most? Is the person serious? Frivolous?

From understanding a person's values and grounding in life, it is a short step away to refer to the Saturn finger as the money finger, as we do in the new system. Money, and our skill in handling its challenges and opportunities, very much reflects our values and conscience. Because the back of the hand represents the real world, and because money "makes the world go around," this finger stands for money. Money is the currency that defines much of our action in the world.

Apollo, the ringer finger, is associated with joy and creativity. These luminous qualities are best expressed in relationships with others, particularly a mate. And interestingly enough, in a deeply and unconsciously held belief, the ring finger has always been associated with relationships, reserved as it is for the wedding ring.

The new view of the back of the fingers accepts this popular wisdom, and designates the ring finger as the relationship finger.

Mercury, the little finger, has quite a bit of mobility on the hand. Mercury, in myth, is the winged messenger, and fleet of foot. Mercury is traditionally read as a business finger, and that is quite fitting. One needs to be quick on the draw, not letting any grass grow underfoot, to be successful in business and to stay ahead of the competition. One has to be as shrewd as Mercury, who could size up any situation in a flash and turn it to his advantage.

No one would deny the importance of business in the everyday world. What may not have come to everyone's attention is the fact that everything we do, on some level, is a matter of business. But because the word "business" normally means a formal arrangement, an office, and a cash payback, we will need another word to express the role of the little finger, in the view from the back of the hand.

Rather than call the little finger business, we substitute the word "negotiation." All life is a matter of negotiation, when we interact on an sustained level with other people. Negotiation does include the concept of business. But negotiation can refer to any activity, from buying a million-dollar home, to getting your child to go to bed on time without an actual cash bribe!

Here is a list to show the comparison between the two ways of naming the fingers.

STANDARD		NEW VIEW	
Finger	**Name**	**Finger**	**Name**
Index	Jupiter: Leadership	Index	Career finger
Middle	Saturn: Values	Middle	Money finger
Ring	Apollo: Creativity	Ring	Relationship finger
Little	Mercury: Business	Little	Negotiation finger

In both systems, the thumb does not have a special name, but remains simply "the thumb." That is not to undervalue the thumb, but only serves to emphasize the fact that its function is different. Rather than represent a specific function in the world, the thumb stands for the human will, as it is applied to all situations.

In the new system, the thumb can be used, at first glance, to help time the body language of the

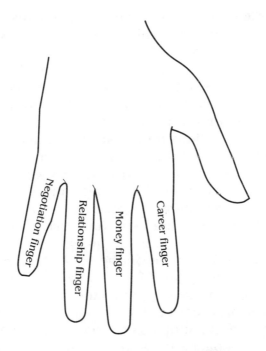

hand. But that use is apart from the steps to be taken with the knuckles. It is interesting to note here that only the four fingers on each hand are used to interpret the knuckles.

This is due to the structure of the thumb itself. As the hands are stretched out, palms down, on a tabletop surface, only the four fingers lie flat, facing outward, toward the person who will interpret them. The position of the thumb, designed to oppose the other fingers, makes it lie sideways and out of view when the hands are placed palms down.

A glance at the length of the thumb and its outside surface will readily reveal that there is only one knuckle with the ridges and lines which can be interpreted. This joint divides the tip from the middle section. The other knuckle joins the thumb to the hand itself. This knuckle does not have the lines and ridges.

When we come to name the knuckles, each of the four sets, we do not have the precedent we do with the fingers. We will not be referring to the gods and their roles in myth.

Their actions took place in a timeless space of humanity's memory. The action of the knuckles, related as it is directly to the real world, can take place only in time, not apart from it. In fact, the knuckles are named precisely according to their role in representing time, and revealing the conditions of the past, present, and future.

The role of time on the back of the hands is to give our everyday life a context. What we were conscious of having experienced and are still conscious of experiencing, has an order to it. The names of the knuckles reflect this order.

Let's pause for a minute and think about the order used to tell a story. If your life were a novel, how would you tell the story? Begin at the beginning of whatever you wish to tell. You do not have to describe your whole life, that's not required; what you must do is present your story so it makes sense.

This is true for the knuckles, too. How do we organize their story? Through the time frames on each set of knuckles and the role of the knuckles in a part of your life which determines their names.

The names for the four sets of knuckles are:

1. The first set, the middle knuckles on the nondominant hand, are called the **background knuckles.**

2. The second set, the tip knuckles on the nondominant hand, are called the **catalyst knuckles.**

3. The third set, the middle knuckles on the dominant hand, are called the **present knuckles.**

4. The fourth set, the tip knuckles on the dominant hand, are called the **future knuckles.**

Ideally, the first and second sets of knuckles tell us something of the past that shapes current issues. The purpose of the first set of knuckles is to give the background details of a situation related to various areas of your life. The role of the second set is to show what events from the last six months will act as a catalyst to our future. The third set, the present knuckles, focuses on current events and issues in various areas of our lives. The fourth set, the future knuckles, predicts an outcome to present concerns.

So, using the four sets of knuckles, we learn about a situation in the order it has occurred, how it is progressing, and what its outcome will be.

The diagram on the following page will show you clearly how to label the knuckles. Refer to this diagram until you have the order memorized.

Knowing these names for the knuckles helps us understand the role of each knuckle on each finger. We can get the background, the catalyst for current and expected developments, a look at the present, and a view of the future for the story each finger contains: details of our career on the index finger; about our money on the middle finger; about our relationships from our ring finger; and

the life we set up for ourselves, through our negotiations, on our little finger.

It's a thorough and orderly miniature world
that we find in the knuckles, a world that is complete and comprehensible, if only we have the keys
to it. Names are the keys.

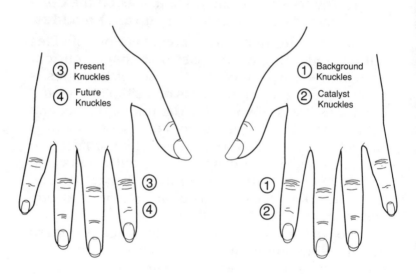

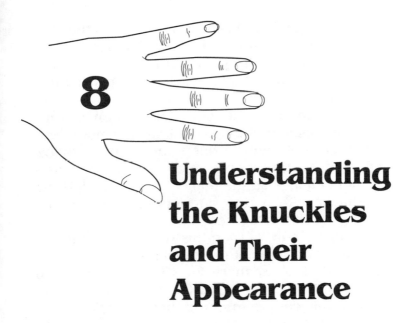

8

Understanding the Knuckles and Their Appearance

With the knuckles' appearance, we come to an exciting aspect of the new way to look at hands — the visual! We have already seen that the knuckles are the centerpiece of the back of the hands. Their shape, color, and lines hold clues to our world and our future.

The most demanding feature of the knuckles, the lines, is the most intriguing. For the lines in the knuckles are really "lines plus," because they are not only straight lines, but form images and symbols.

All of palmistry is a visual art, but no part of it is more visual than the world of the knuckles. The features and images are concentrated. Looking at knuckles over a period of time, watching how the images form and change, seems very much like looking at a tiny television screen. It's rather fun to ask people to "see their television screens" ... and that is not entirely a joke, for the images in the knuckles do change, just as images on a screen move.

The images on a television screen change within seconds; the images in knuckles not nearly that often, not even in one sitting. But to follow their progress throughout a period of months, seeing them change as the reality around the individual changes is exciting, and lets you feel you are viewing the drama of life.

Your keys to viewing this drama are found in the shape and color of the knuckles, as well as the lines. Let's look at these keys for a minute, and understand how they work. In the following chapters, we will learn to interpret these keys.

REASON FOR THE KNUCKLES' SHAPE

As we saw in Chapter 2, shape in the knuckles refers to the skin on top of the joints themselves. That skin can and does arrange itself into different patterns.

But what causes the shape to differ in knuckles? Shape varies in the knuckles not only from person to person, but also from knuckle to knuckle, for the same person.

Such selective shape must mean something. To find out, we need to know what the shape represents. There is a very good analogy to explain what the shape is, and what causes it. You need only to think of a face, in its expression and movements, of a smile, or a frown. The knuckles' shape is the same as an expression on a face. A face's expression transmits what a person is feeling. The expression may be momentary or longer lasting. A bit of good news or an unexpected annoyance bring on an expression that registers what the person feels.

Longer lasting expressions form a habitual look to the face. An ecstatic pair of newlyweds will look radiant through the early days of their marriage. On the contrary, continual worry or constant negative emotions cause a face to fall into drooping lines or a harsh look.

These states of mind can change, and as they do, the habitual set of the face also changes — from happy to sad, or from harsh to smooth, as circumstances change. The characteristic expression reflects a person's ongoing orientation to life.

The appearance of the skin as it covers the knuckles expresses exactly the same thing. A smooth knuckle is the equivalent of a smile; a bumpy knuckle with raised ridges or dents is the same as a frown.

Experience and a person's response to it cause the face and the knuckles to look the way they do. One could say, "But heredity accounts for the way a face looks." Yes it can, in the features; even the states of mind that produce the flickering expressions in those features can be hereditary. Not surprisingly, heredity plays a role in the shape of the knuckles as well. Certain shapes are found on parent-child teams frequently.

A further point could be made: a person's health also influences how the face will look. Health, in the sense of vitality and positive response to life, is also shown in the knuckles.

Our habitual response to life, and the way our experience conditions us, accounts for the knuckle shape. It's very simple. The phrase "happy life, happy face" can be exchanged for "smooth life, smooth knuckles."

No knuckle shape is entirely permanent. The cumulative effect of our experience creates the current shape in our knuckles.

When we study the various knuckle shapes and their interpretation in Chapters 9 to 13, you will see the application for the "frown" or "smile" theory in greater detail.

REASON FOR THE KNUCKLES' COLOR

The knuckles' color is a remarkable feature, and the cause of the various shades of color in a knuckle is even more intriguing. The knuckles' color and images are simply a printout of things you know about your future on an unconscious level. You have the information about your future; you simply cannot access it at will.

With the knuckles' color, you can get a preview of how many current situations will turn out.

The principle behind this is quite simple. Like the shape, color is related to the appearance of a face. When your cheeks are pink or your skin has a glow to it, you know you're healthy. When, on the contrary, your face is pale and haggard-looking, you know you aren't feeling your best.

When you are under the weather, how are you going to do your job? You are not going to be able to perform as well as you can when you are feeling great. Pink in the face is a clue that you are on "all systems go," and a very pale color alerts you — and the world — that this is not one of your better days, and that your momentum is going to be slow.

Color shades in the knuckles work on the very same principle. Pink or shiny tones are a "go" signal, and the tiny areas that are pale are a "slow" signal. Think of pink as a positive momentum signal, and pale as a negative momentum signal.

Negative momentum does not mean a negative event, but simply that the situation described by the lines in the knuckle will have a difficult or slow outcome. Again, you can do your job with the flu and the pale face it causes, you just can't do it as fast or efficiently as usual.

Color in a face reflects a body's state of well-being or lack of it. In knuckles, color reflects an unconscious awareness of the future, of how situations over a short period of time will work out.

Unconscious knowledge that things are going to go well causes the blood vessels to dilate, just as a sudden pleasure can make the face flush.

An unconscious awareness of a difficult future makes the flow of blood constrict in the knuckle, producing a pale color, just as receiving a shock can make the vessels contract and restrict the blood flow to the face.

These contrasting colors in a knuckle are subtle. The reaction is not as big or noticeable as in
the face, but the principle is the same, because the
blood flow is similar.

The secret to color in the fingers is that the
blood flow to the fingers is similar to the circulation in a face. The nerves in the face are highly
developed and require a good flow of blood to
nourish them. The same is true of fingers, and
especially the knuckles, which have a great deal of
mobility. Interestingly, an expressive face is often
called "mobile."

We will see how the colors in a knuckle are
used to predict success in Chapters 14 and 15.

REASON FOR THE
KNUCKLES' LINES

The revealing color in our knuckles comes from an
unconscious awareness of our future. Further
details about the future are found in the images
and symbols in the knuckles that the lines form.
The brain records and prints out this information in
the form of lines and images. How is it that the
brain has this knowledge and bothers to record it
in the knuckles?

The brain is a monitor whose job is to keep us
alive. To do this, the brain first regulates our bodies' functions, our heart rate, our respiration, and
all the systems that sustain us. As an extension of
this job, the brain reaches out, on a level that is as
unconscious and automatic as its maintenance of

our bodies, and searches our environment for clues to anything that will impact us and our well-being.

The brain today continues to scan our environment just as it did in the earliest days. When humankind first stepped out of the cave, the world around was unknown and threatening. The brain was alert for any signal of danger. And certainly the early world held fewer variables to contend with than our world today. The brain has continually adapted to its increased work load in its function as a monitor of our external world.

Like a computer, our brain stores all the information it gathers about the world surrounding us. And as our world is far-flung, and our every association is potentially significant, the brain keeps track of people around us and their role in our lives. Is the world safe or not? Are people friendly or a threat? The brain knows it all, and guides us as best it can.

In the early days of humanity, the brain was alert to signs of physical danger, and gave us the quick reflexes necessary to avoid it. The brain does that today, and has expanded its protective role to include an awareness of social, emotional, and psychological factors that influence our lives.

All of this information is recorded in the knuckles, in a primitive language of images and symbols. Already recognized as the simple and universal language of dreams and the unconscious, symbols are also an ingredient in the silent world of the knuckles. The body carries the imprint of what the brain knows.

This concept should not be startling, after a moment's thought. That the body reflects much of our inner being, our health and emotions, is an accepted fact. Medicine recognizes the link between mental, emotional, and physical well-being. It's just that the role of the knuckles as a reflection of our inner knowledge of the external world takes the concept a step further.

The knuckles are a tiny portion of the whole body, but they are our windows on the world; a new territory entirely overlooked and ready for exploration.

To be familiar with a person's world and the way he or she has adapted to it, we have only to read these three clues: the shape, the color, and lines in the knuckles.

The following chart summarizes the causes for the knuckles' appearance.

Feature	Cause
Shape	Our life experience and how it has conditioned us to respond to life. What we expect based on past encounters.
Color	The unconscious awareness of how events in life will turn out.
Lines	Describe the world around us. The brain keeps track of this reality as part of its job of ensuring survival.

CHANGES IN THE FEATURES OF THE KNUCKLES

What makes these features in the knuckles so compelling is that they change over a period of time. How could they not, if they reflect our world and changing fortunes?

How often do these features change? Can we see the changes taking place? We rarely see the changes as they happen, because changes in the features of the knuckles work on exactly the same basis as other changes in the body's appearance. The minute fluctuations of a body from hour to hour, and from day to day, go unnoticed. A ten-pound weight gain or loss does not occur in one day. Changes in the body's appearance are cumulative until enough has altered to create a noticeable difference.

So, how long until we can see a difference in the knuckles?

Feature	Time to change
Shape	6 months to a year or more
Lines	3 months
Color	Weeks

Because the cause for the knuckles' changing shape is the cumulative effect of our experiences, changes in shape do not happen often. At the most dramatic, a change might occur within six months. This means a person has had a drastic change in circumstances and has adjusted enough to record the difference. A more moderate period of time is one or more years for a change to take place.

Because the world itself changes rapidly, and the addition of a single detail in our lines — a new friend, a marriage, a baby, a job — can alter much of our future, the lines change frequently. In one instance, a set of lines was seen to change overnight. But experience and research show that for enough time to elapse, to allow enough of the images to change, and a different story to emerge (sometimes the sequel to an earlier tale!), three months is a minimum requirement.

To understand how often color changes, think of the variables in our lives as billiard balls arranged on a table. The impact of one ball on another can start a chain reaction that changes the dynamics of the whole picture. This is what a single event can do to our prospective fortunes. For this reason, color in the knuckles is constantly updated, to keep track of the new possibilities created by the clash of variables.

Weeks are the normal time frame for any change in color. However, if conditions stay constant, so does the color.

That's the fun of it! You never know what's happening until you check it all out, using the changing features in the knuckles.

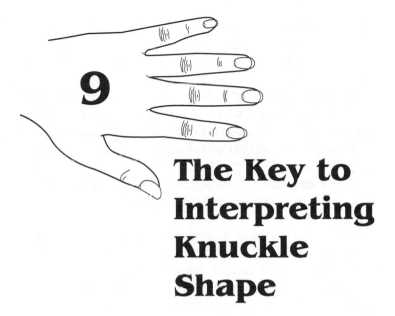

9

The Key to Interpreting Knuckle Shape

How do you feel about your life? At times we all question whether our lives are really as easy or as difficult as we imagine. If we look to the outside for others' opinions, or compare their lives to our own, we still don't know how to evaluate our lives as objectively as we would like, if we are in a mood to question them.

What if you could have an instant record that answers your question? The knuckles' shape does exactly that. The relative long-term ease or stress of our lives shows up clearly in knuckle shape.

The knuckles' shapes record our experience. How has life treated us? Well? Not well? Have we had to struggle? Have we sailed through? Furthermore, how will we respond to our next experiences? Do we expect success, or do we expect struggle? Whatever we expect, we only anticipate the reality we already know.

The knuckles' shape not only reveals the effect of all past experience, but the way we anticipate the future. Because our experience and mindset have much to say about our future and its happiness, understanding the result of life's twists and turns by interpreting knuckle shape can help us prepare for and deal well with the future.

The knuckles' shape can point out areas of life that are satisfactory, and those that need work on our part.

In this first look at knuckle shape, we will concentrate only on the middle knuckles. These knuckles have a larger area of skin on them that arranges itself into any of six shapes when the fingers are extended and held straight.

First, the shapes. Middle knuckles can have any of these patterns:

1. Smooth
2. Raised and average to the touch
3. Raised and firm to the touch
4. Raised and soft to the touch
5. Dented
6. Furrowed

These patterns on the knuckles can be determined in the following manner.

Smooth knuckles: The skin stretches across the knuckles smoothly, and the skin is flat across the knuckle, with no raised ridges or bumps.

Raised and average to the touch: The skin ridges bulge up in a little pad. The raised area can

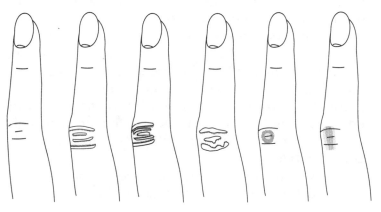

Smooth   Raised   Raised/   Raised/   Dented   Furrowed
                      firm   soft

Knuckle shapes

cover the whole knuckle or part of it. The skin on the knuckle, when touched, has average resistance to it, just as a palm with a medium consistency does.

Raised and firm to the touch: The skin ridges bulge up, and when touched, feel rock hard, resisting an attempt to push them in.

Raised and soft to the touch: The skin ridges bulge up, and when touched, cave right in, feeling squishy to the touch. A knuckle with this soft quality to the skin will also appear whiter (where skin color allows this) than the rest of the finger. A white look to a raised knuckle alerts you, even before you touch it, that the knuckle surface will be soft. The skin sometimes resembles a blister.

Dented knuckles: The skin on the knuckle looks as if it has a hole punched in it. The outside edges will be raised, rather like a donut, with a hole in the center. This look is so distinctive you will not miss it when you see it.

Furrowed knuckles: The skin on the knuckles in this type is also sunken in, but the shape is not circular. Instead, the shape is long and vertical, covering the length of the knuckle. This shape looks like a rut or a tire track impressed into the knuckle. This shape can also be called a trough because it is a deep indentation that looks as if it could be filled.

Now that you can identify these shapes, your first question will be, "But what do they mean?"

Shape	Meaning
Smooth	A good attitude, optimistic. A smooth path in life. Easy circumstances.
Raised and average	Knowledgeable. Experienced. Busy life.
Raised and firm	Confident. Successful. Accomplishments. Positive experiences.
Raised and soft	Indecisive. Often feels overwhelmed. Challenges, complex experiences, disappointments.
Dented	Feels the pressures of life. Tense. Alert. Difficult moments.
Furrowed	Feels stuck. Needs to raise self-esteem. Hard work. Efforts unrewarded.

A smooth knuckle means experience has made a person's way easier, and that success is very likely. A raised knuckle of any type shows an extra dose of "experience," and is found on people who have a high profile in their jobs or creative lives. Firm raised ridges act as a "toner," revealing a "workout" in life experience. A firm raised ridge is a sign of "fitness" for life. Soft raised ridges, while they show a lot of experience, also reveal disappointment or complex experiences which demand a lot of the person. At times the person does not feel up to these demands, as if he or she were a little "out of shape." A dented appearance to the knuckle represents the "knocks of life" a person has felt, and portrays feelings of frustration, as does a furrowed knuckle. The difference between a dented and furrowed knuckle is that the furrowed knuckle specifically shows a lack of reward for effort put out. A little bit like staying faithfully on a diet, and not losing the expected pounds.

A person with a smooth set of knuckles expects to succeed. A person with average raised ridges is confident he or she can handle anything that comes up. A person with firm raised ridges expects to get ahead constantly and to have an active, exciting life. With soft raised ridges, a person looks for "trouble," is cautious, patient, and willing to endure complex situations. With dents, a person expects life to be challenging, to feel as if it is pressing in and asking for the impossible. At times this expectation acts as a tonic, urging the person toward achievement; at other times, the same expectation can make a person feel irritable or depressed. A person with furrowed knuckles certainly feels overwhelmed and does not always expect others to understand this. Thus, this person often does not ask enough of others, often preferring to sit, to wait and tough it out.

Now that you know the shapes of the middle knuckles and their meanings, here is how you can apply them.

To the knuckles as a whole: Are the middle knuckles on both of your hands mostly the same shape, or all the same shape? If so, then you can read them simply, using the meaning of the shape that applies, remembering to distinguish between your nondominant and your dominant hands.

The shape on the nondominant hand shows your past experience and how it has affected you. The shape on your dominant hand reveals your prospects based on present conditions.

You can review the meanings of these two sets (1 and 3) of the knuckles in Chapter 7, if you have any questions on the differences in timing between the two hands.

To the knuckles on each individual finger: You can chart your progress in life, finger by finger, using the meanings for each individual finger. Your index fingers represent your career; your middle fingers, your money; your ring fingers, your relationships; your little fingers, your negotiating skills.

As you look at both of your career fingers, both of your money fingers, and both of your relationship and negotiating skill fingers, you will either find that their shapes are the same, or they are not. If they are the same, read the past and present prospects as the same.

If the knuckle shapes on each set of fingers are different, the meanings are applied according to the hand on which the shape is found. The shape of your career finger, for instance, on your nondominant hand reveals how your past career experience has set you up for the future; the shape of the middle knuckles on the dominant hand shows how the current trends in your career will affect the future of your career.

Contrasting shapes: If the shapes are different for a set of fingers, whether the finger is the index, middle, ring, or little finger, the meanings take a little longer to figure out and apply. For this reason, the next four chapters are devoted to that study.

For now, we are going to continue with the meanings of the shapes applied to the knuckles overall, and to each individual finger. These meanings are less complicated than the contrasting meanings, and should be learned as the beginning steps in understanding knuckle shape.

All knuckles smooth: Life has a lucky feel about it for you, most of the time. You do not often feel overwhelmed by details, and you expect the best. Your optimistic and confident nature comes from the fact that life has taught you that you get what you aim for. Your motto: "No problem!"

All knuckles raised and average: You rise to the challenge, every time. You like situations that make you stretch and grow. You have experienced human behavior at its best and its worst. Because you know a great deal about life, you are prepared to meet your experiences head on. You know when to do battle and when to retreat, accepting life on its own terms. Your motto: "A man — or woman — of the world!"

All knuckles raised and firm: Experience is a valuable teacher for you. Life offers many opportunities and you know how to turn them into gold. You are used to sweeping away obstacles, and are perfectly capable of planning a future that meets your dreams and expectations; a future that unfolds according to your desire and vision. Your motto: "Let's go for it!"

All knuckles raised and soft: Your world seems wobbly at times. You have had your share of sadness and disappointment, and life has taught you not to trust too deeply in its flow or in people until you have done your homework. You feel a need to double check everything, and to keep on top of details. You can dither, make certain decisions, then undo them and start over. You are simply taking the long road rather than the shortcut. There is light at the end of the tunnel, and your troubles all seem to have a special or unexpected benefit in the end. Your motto: "Nobody knows the trouble I've seen."

All knuckles dented: Dents in your knuckles are proof that the world has made its mark on you, not the reverse! Ideally, you will someday reciprocate and make your mark on the world. Your willpower, sense of duty, and determination keep you in places where others might escape or just give up. Take that determination, combine it with a small amount of inspiration, and find new resolutions for the pressures you have. You long to escape from the constant pressures in your life. You can, with even perhaps so much as a new viewpoint. Your motto: "On the whole, I'd rather be in Acapulco."

All knuckles furrowed: These ruts in your knuckles are evidence of the straight and narrow path, the long journey and extra miles you have undertaken to make your life — or, often, someone else's — all you think it should be. You are now puzzled at the lack of return for your efforts and wonder what to do next. Run, don't walk, to the nearest exit, and find the magic door marked as the entrance to a new life, a life in which you feel freer, even if even if you can't act freer — yet! The old saw, "act as if," and the appropriate feelings can be reversed here. You must feel freer inside yourself to do what you want to do. The rest will follow. Your motto: "Liberation now!"

Now let's look at the meanings of each shape applied to the four areas of life represented by your four fingers.

Shape on the index finger knuckles: Reveals details of your career. Smooth index fingers mean a smooth career path and that you are satisfied with your work. Raised index patterns mean you work hard, you attract others' notice, and you are upwardly mobile. Firm raised index knuckles are a sign of accomplishment, and a confident approach to your work. Soft raised patterns are a sign of challenge and that you are not satisfied with your work. Dented index knuckles reveal unproductive pressures in your career, and that the essentials for success are not in place. Furrowed index knuckles mean your abilities are not recognized or rewarded. Your career focus needs a change.

Shape on the middle finger knuckles: Reveals details of your finances. Smooth middle finger knuckles mean a secure path to financial success, and that you are satisfied with your finances. Average raised ridges show experience at making money. You know the value of money. Firm raised ridges reveal a good financial planner and fundraiser. Soft raised ridges indicate you are challenged by a low pay scale, or confused about how best to get ahead financially. Dented knuckles show you work hard for money and carry a few financial burdens. With furrowed knuckles, efforts at financial security have not paid off. You must change your money focus — earn more or spend less, and restructure your priorities.

Shape on the ring finger knuckles: Reveals details of your relationships. Smooth ring finger knuckles mean personal relationships are satisfying and successful. Average raised knuckles mean you understand human nature well, and are experienced at dealing with people. Firm raised ridges show a real "people person," successful at working with the public. Soft raised ridges reveal confusion and uncertainty about others' actions, and a tenderhearted person. Dented knuckles mean pressure in relationships, and that you must have more freedom to fulfill your personal needs. Furrowed knuckles reveal an element of strain in relationships that erodes your sense of self-worth. You need to be aware of deserving more. Reserve some care and attention for yourself.

Shape on the little finger knuckles: Reveals details of your negotiating ability. Smooth little finger knuckles mean an excellent ability to negotiate, and satisfaction in the achievement of large and small goals. Average raised ridges mean you understand "the ways of the world," and make deals successfully. Firm raised ridges reveal a superior ability to negotiate, gained from personal experience. Soft raised ridges indicate you are bothered by a lack of achievement of one or more goals. You are willing to try a new route to success. Dented knuckles show unexpected setbacks in your projects, which get you down. You can outwit the opposition by taking an unexpected route yourself, then going for your goal again. Furrowed knuckles mean you have tried to accomplish more than is possible. Redesign your goals and projects to give you more realistic and immediate satisfaction.

QUICK CHECK

Here is a tip for success for each knuckle shape. Each shape merits specific advice.

Smooth knuckles: You're doing it right. Keep on with the way you normally do things.

Average raised: Put yourself out there and you will get ahead.

Firm raised: Use the real gains you have made to go even further.

Soft raised: Don't be discouraged, just forge ahead.

Dented: Do what it takes to cancel the pressures that block you now.

Furrowed: Rearrange your priorities, knowing that you deserve success.

CONTRASTING KNUCKLE SHAPES

If the shape of one finger's knuckle is different, depending on which hand it is found, the contrasting shapes give more details about the person's path to success in the area of life the finger represents.

Using the different shapes on a set of knuckles, whether it is the index, middle, ring, or little finger knuckles, we can review a person's past experience and compare that with the present prospects. In the next four chapters, we will explore the meanings for these contrasting shapes.

Do not be concerned about applying these contrasting shapes until you are comfortable with the meaning of each shape: first, in itself; second, as applied to each hand. The last step is to apply the meanings to each knuckle on each finger of each hand. If you do not want to memorize these meanings now, skip ahead to the chapter on color. Later, when you have questions about the meaning of a contrasting set of finger shapes, you will have a handy reference in the next four chapters.

Finger	Shape	Meaning/Impact
Index	Smooth	Smooth path to career; satifaction with work
	Raised	Works hard; attracts other's notice; upward mobility
	Raised/firm	Sign of accomplishment; confident approach to work

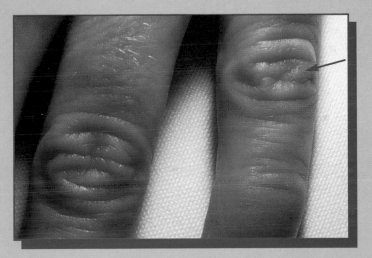

Double fish symbol, little finger,
noses touching

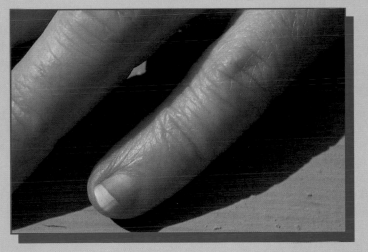

Triangular head

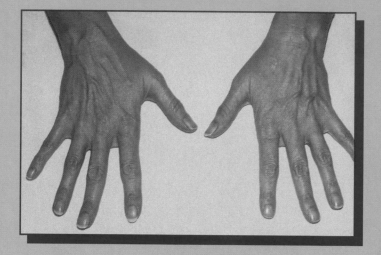

Furrowed ridge

Warrior on palm, on Mars Mount
(Beside thumb on the right)

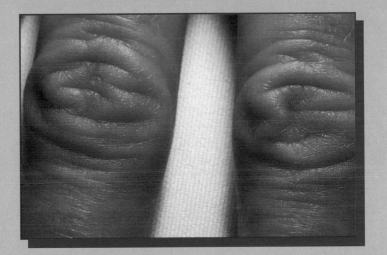

Soft raised ridges

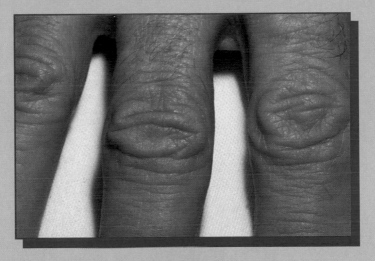

Firm raised ridges

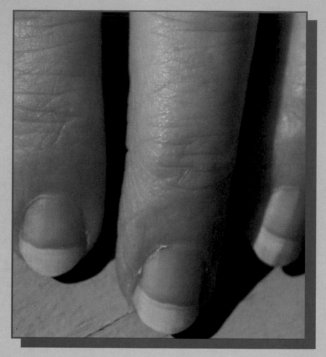

Middle finger tip knuckle has two
puffy figures in profile

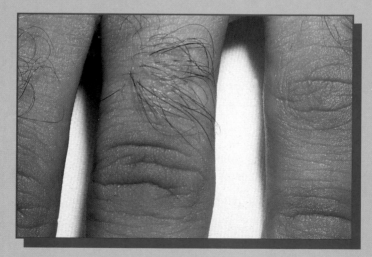

Extra shine on dark skin

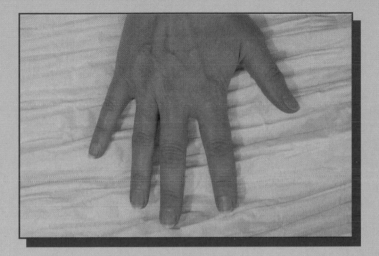

Pink knuckles

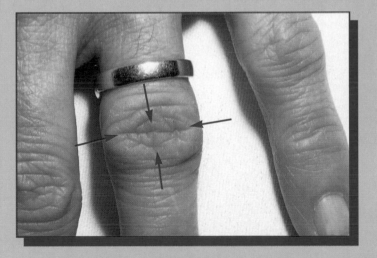

Group of abstract warrior figures

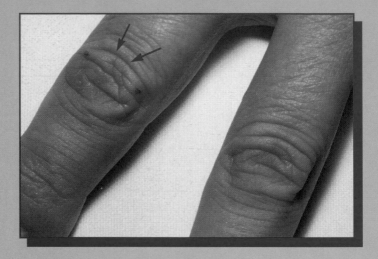

Two warriors, with arms linked

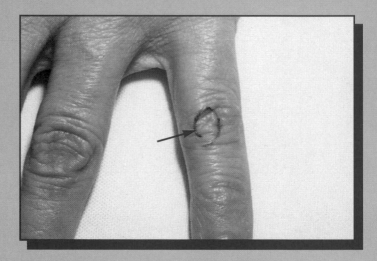

Warrior circled in black ink

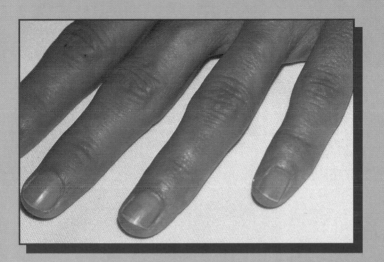

Smooth knuckles

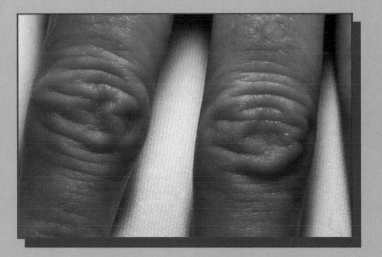

Dented knuckles

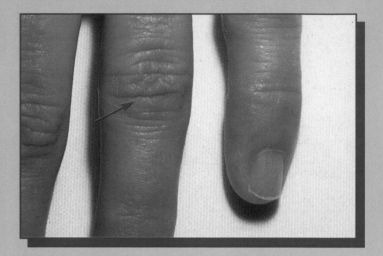

Mountain symbol

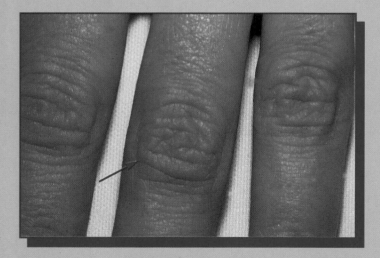

Warrior on ring finger,
middle knuckle, center left

Finger	Shape	Meaning/Impact
Index	Raised/soft	Sign of challenges; not satisfied with work
	Dented	Unproductive pressures in career; essentials for sucess not in place
	Furrowed	Abilities not recognized or rewarded; career focus needs a change
Middle	Smooth	Path to financial success secure
	Raised	Experienced at making money; knows the value of money
	Raised/firm	Good fundraiser; excellent financial planning ability
	Raised/soft	Challenged by low pay scale; confused about how best to get ahead financially
	Dented	Works hard for money; carries financial burdens
	Furrowed	Efforts at financial security have not paid off; possibly entrenched in debt; must change money focus; earn more or spend less; restructure priorities

Finger	Shape	Meaning/Impact
Ring	Smooth	Personal relationships are satisfying and successful
	Raised	Understands human nature well; experience at dealing with people
	Raised/firm	A real "people person"; success at working with the public
	Raised/soft	Confused and unsure about others' actions; tenderhearted
	Dented	Feels pressure in relationships; must have more freedom and fulfill personal needs
	Furrowed	Element of strain in relationships erodes self-worth; needs to be aware of deserving more; reserve some attention for self
Little	Smooth	Excellent ability to negotiate; satisfaction in the achievement of large and small goals
	Raised	Understands "the ways of the world"; makes deals successfully
	Raised/firm	Superior ability to negotiate, gained from personal experience

Finger	Shape	Meaning/Impact
Little	Raised/soft	Bothered by lack of achievement of one or more goals; willing to try a new route to success
	Dented	Unexpected setbacks in your projects get you down; you can out-wit the opposition by taking an unexpected route yourself, then going for your goal again
	Furrowed	You have tried to accomplish more than is possible; redesign goals and projects to give you more realistic and immediate satis-faction

CONTRASTING KNUCKLE SHAPES

The contrast in knuckle shape from finger to finger gives insight into past experience and present prospects. The middle knuckles on the nondominant hand show long-term or cumulative experience, and on the dominant hand, the present prospects. Using these two sets of knuckles, we get the background information about a situation, and see where that background has led the person, up to the present moment.

This information is made possible by the fact that the role of each hand is different. Each hand represents a different phase of experience. The meanings of the shapes are the same. Applying these meanings to different time frames is the first step to grasping the story of a person's life.

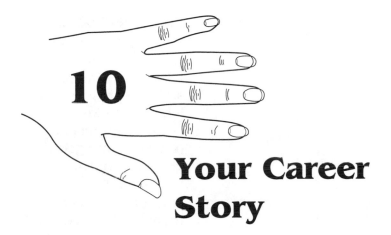

10

Your Career Story

To follow the record of your career as it is recorded in your index finger middle knuckle shapes, compare the shape of the knuckle on the nondominant hand with the shape of the knuckle on the dominant hand. The contrast in the shape tells how your career has developed over the last year or two, and where it is heading, based on current indications.

In the following chart, "ND" means the middle knuckle on the index finger of the nondominant hand, and "D" refers to the middle knuckle on the index finger of the dominant hand.

ND	D	**Career indications**
Smooth	Smooth	You are clear about your career goals. Past achievements and satisfying results have led you to expect success. Your present prospects are good; expect advances in your career.
Smooth	Raised	Your past achievements and success are significant and have led directly to a higher profile and level of responsibility. You demand results and you get them.
Smooth	Raised/firm	You like your work. No hours are too long, no task too small. Your appetite for variety in your work has given you a wide range of experience, a stepping stone to top performance.

ND	D	**Career indications**
Smooth	Raised/soft	You have been lucky in your past experience. Your experience did not teach you to expect the roadblocks which now arise. Stay focused, use the skills you know best, and be patient. Your past record will help you succeed, in spite of a current setback.
Smooth	Dented	You have seen brighter days at work in the past. Do not let current conditions upset you or emotionally "black-mail" you. Do the work you can now. Revise your resumé and talk to friends and advisers who know the market for your skills. Your experience will make you a good player in the right company.

ND	**D**	**Career indications**
Smooth	Furrowed	You've really been in the swing of things at work in the past. You know what success feels like. When did the tide turn? Was it a new boss, a new employee? Fatigue? Boredom? When something about work no longer feels good, why not change it, even if you chuck the whole thing? There's a job for you that can give you all the fun and hope of the old days.
Raised	Smooth	Your past work experience is substantial and sets you up to make the most of current favorable career conditions.
Raised	Raised	Your past work record reveals your outstanding skills. You are in a unique position to make gains in your career now.

ND	**D**	**Career indications**
Raised	Raised/firm	Your past track record offers you an opportunity for expansion of your goals in the present. Success is yours.
Raised	Raised/soft	You have won your laurels in the past. But past rewards do not seem to be the bridge to success under current work conditions. Analyze the weak points in your career; change those under your control to gain a more advantageous position.
Raised	Dented	You often think about past achievements and wonder if they are the key to the future. Your training and experiences are unequal to the pressures of the moment. Consider new training or find a way to use skills you have but currently do not use in your work.

ND	D	Career indications
Raised	Furrowed	Past success makes frustrations a puzzle. How did you get to this point? You have the keys to a more rewarding work style. Back off, and pretend you are a stranger at your desk and work environment. What would you do differently? Objectivity helps you find an answer.
Raised/firm	Smooth	You have hit the heights in your past career experience; having achieved at least one pinnacle, you are set to begin yet another path to success.
Raised/firm	Raised	You have had a peak career experience and laid the foundation for current success. Others ask your advice.
Raised/firm	Raised/firm	There is no higher potential record of success than these two knuckles. You have the advantage in your dealings and can shape your future success along the lines that satisfy you most.

ND	D	Career indications
Raised/firm	Raised/soft	"What goes up must come down" — or so you must feel, because you've hit a snag in your career plans. Carefully check all ventures you are considering. You will find their flaws because experience has taught you what works and what does not.
Raised/firm	Dented	You know how success works — you've been there long enough to see the ups and downs of a chosen career. You have the skills to combat the challenges you face. Remove any pressures; scale down the amount of your work, if necessary, to get a new perspective.
Raised/firm	Furrowed	Where have all the rewards of yesterday gone? You are feeling trounced in every corner of your career. Why put up with this? Complete one task at a time and get the rewards, however large or small, now!

ND	**D**	**Career indications**
Raised/soft	Smooth	In the past, you accepted challenges in your work. You were patient in your approach to problems, and confident you would see your way through. You have won! Changes made bring success.
Raised/soft	Raised	What a switch! Just when you thought you were stagnating in your career, you had a lucky break. You were no slouch. You saw your chance and took it. The future looks good.
Raised/soft	Raised/firm	Whew! Your relief knows no bounds. Now that the past slump is over, you have a new set of opportunities and you are making the most of them.
Raised/soft	Raised/soft	Sluggish conditions in your career are troublesome. You are still not sure how best to proceed, but you are slowly being pushed to realize something has to give. You are ready for a change.

ND	D	Career indications
Raised/soft	Dented	You thought last year's work conditions were bad. Now you have an added pressure, which is a blessing in disguise, because it starts you on a new path. Prepare for the next step, because it will lead to more productive work.
Raised/soft	Furrowed	Work conditions have been a problem. You are just now getting in touch with the fact that you need more reward and recognition for your skills. With this awareness, a turning point is at hand.
Dented	Smooth	In the last year or two, you put up with pressures at work that have now been resolved. You have learned what a successful career takes, and you are using this knowledge effectively to set a new standard for yourself.

ND	D	Career indications
Dented	Raised	You are on your way, having shed the old annoyances that threatened to surround you indefinitely. Success lies ahead.
Dented	Raised/firm	You feel reborn! Nothing like a change in prospects to inspire your best efforts. Your career has had night and day swings, and at the moment, you are in line for the jackpot.
Dented	Raised/soft	Last year you were focused on different issues at work. You felt pressure and restraints in particular situations. Now you seem to sense you're not alone in your challenges. Company atmosphere needs overhauling.
Dented	Dented	An old saying comes to mind: "When the going gets tough, the tough get going." You are about to release past and present pressures. If sufficiently focused, your strategy can work.

ND	**D**	**Career indications**
Dented	Furrowed	In the past. when events got you down, you never dreamed problems could last so long. You are in a mood to forge ahead or retreat — whichever seems practical. Spend time mapping options.
Furrowed	Smooth	After a year of discouraging conditions in your career, you have regained your options. Now you can build your career in line with your dreams.
Furrowed	Raised	When you felt the day of "light at the end of the tunnel" would never arrive, it did; you are making the most of revived career prospects. You are in line for advancement.
Furrowed	Raised/firm	You know how far hope and tenacity in the face of adversity have brought you. Yesterday's woes are today's gains. Congratulations on the new expansion of your career potential.

ND	D	Career indications
Furrowed	Raised/soft	You have come to understand that slow days at work are not under your control. But you cannot linger in your present circumstances. Enlist the help of a coworker; redefine your role at work.
Furrowed	Dented	When conditions seemed sluggish at work this past year, you hoped for a key to understand your options. The current pressures are that key, offering a way out of a tight spot, and a push toward new options.
Furrowed	Furrowed	Company conditions out of your control make you crazy. You have worked very hard and now feel the strain of the uneven equation: work more, enjoy it less. Now is the time to put your foot down and ask for more for yourself, even if this means a new job for you.

11

Your Money Story

To follow the record of your money as it is recorded in your middle finger middle knuckle shapes, compare the shape of the knuckle on the nondominant hand with the shape of the knuckle on the dominant hand. The contrast in shape reveals how your finances have developed over the last year or two, and where they are heading, based on current indications.

In the following chart, "ND" means the middle knuckle on the middle finger of the nondominant hand, and "D" refers to the middle knuckle on the middle finger of the dominant hand.

ND	D	**Financial indications**
Smooth	Smooth	You have a good grasp of financial matters, as past experience has taught you. You can now make money easily and use it well.
Smooth	Raised	Your money sense has brought gains and made financial goals a reality. Success now spurs you on to more financial payback.
Smooth	Raised/firm	Your financial path has always been open to success. This advantage helps you build the financial structure of your dreams.
Smooth	Raised/soft	You have known financial success in the past and used your skills effectively. Use them now to find your way out of a temporary impasse in earning or spending ability.
Smooth	Dented	Your past natural security has given you the skills to defuse current money pressures. Use this opportunity to define the risks you can take, and be confident of future success.

ND	D	Financial indications
Smooth	Furrowed	Solid financial goals in the past gave you peace of mind. Believe in your financial skills now, as you restructure your material priorities.
Raised	Smooth	Past financial security came to you because you worked for it. Now experience makes new gains possible. Go ahead with current plans.
Raised	Raised	You are on the right track in your financial plans. Future expectations will be realized based on today's performance. Your money skills are excellent.
Raised	Raised/firm	Yesterday's gains are tomorrow's pot of gold. You are confident in your ability to gather all the money you need for success. Experience backs you up in your plans.

ND	**D**	**Financial indications**
Raised	Raised/soft	You have been on a financial fast track. You are used to success. A change in direction is no excuse for a loss of confidence. Conditions can be in your favor with fine-tuning of finances now.
Raised	Dented	You have seen good days at the bank. You know how to raise money for any need. The current setback may be a result of goals no longer practical in today's market. Revise your financial plans.
Raised	Furrowed	The sum of your past know-how is greater than the parts of your current sluggish financial conditions. Get going on a new plan for success. You have the right stuff — apply it to a new operation, to get and keep the success that belongs to you.

ND	**D**	**Financial indications**
Raised/firm	Smooth	You really know the ropes when it comes to money. Your financial experience and current skills will lead to increased income. Be on the lookout for new opportunities that are just now taking shape.
Raised/firm	Raised	No one can beat your past experience or your instincts when it comes to making a profit, however large or small. A number of new ventures now will give you an added edge in your financial quest.
Raised/firm	Raised/firm	Your past experience has taught you certain ventures are always ripe for the plucking. You can smell money and enjoy bringing many potential money-making deals to fruition. You can take risks and diversify now.

ND	**D**	**Financial indications**
Raised/firm	Raised/soft	You know how good it feels to have that secure future in the form of a plump bank account. You will have to overlook current cloudy forecasts or slow to pay deals that may not be your first choice, but will pay long-term rewards.
Raised/firm	Dented	A long string of financial successes in the past will see you through a current turning point. You know how money works — make it work for you.
Raised/firm	Furrowed	You have seen the glory days — for yourself or for family and friends — and you are sorely puzzled by new economic conditions that change old prospects. Never mind. There's more money waiting for you when you change your current goals, and keeping an open mind, rearrange priorities to meet the new developments.

ND	D	Financial indications
Raised/soft	Smooth	Where last year you felt challenged to make your money go as far as you would like, current trends are more in your favor. You are poised for new outlets for your money-making ability.
Raised/soft	Raised	You are happiest when you are making money, and the last year has not been your most rewarding. Now you can look forward to helpful conditions on the road to financial success.
Raised/soft	Raised/firm	You are just amazed at the difference a few months can make in financial cycles. Where last year you just kept your head above water, now the coast is clear. Smooth sailing ahead.
Raised/soft	Raised/soft	Last year's slow developments in financial prospects continue. But you know you are in a cycle that affects others, too. Join with friends in moneymaking ideas. There's strength in numbers.

ND	D	Financial indications
Raised/soft	Dented	Challenges on all sides. That's how money matters feel to you. But wait a minute — this new need is not part of last year's cycle. Your focus now gets you out of a particular bind; in the process, all your money potential receives a boost.
Raised/soft	Furrowed	Sometimes it takes the patience of a saint to outwait a cycle that's not to your liking. You are slowly gaining a new perspective which will change your mind about the value of old financial patterns. Tomorrow is a new day for earning opportunities — seize it!
Dented	Smooth	Last year's pressures have miraculously dissolved, and you are free to take up the search for a satisfying income in better circumstances. Stay alert for a new project.

ND	**D**	**Financial indications**
Dented	Raised	When you had a challenge recently, you simply used the more difficult phases of your financial picture to plot a new course. You are now on the track to major improvement in your income.
Dented	Raised/firm	Plan for a reward now after successfully negotiating your way out of an unexpected bump in the road of your finances over a year ago. Your skills, coupled with newly favorable markets and promising outlets, lead to a fresh round of achievement.
Dented	Raised/soft	You had to cope with a particular challenge in the past, in order to keep yourself afloat financially. Now you must make sure slow conditions or lack of income do not cause your level of living and spending to take a dive. Create your own style apart from the mainstream.

ND	D	**Financial indications**
Dented	Dented	Problems and more problems. After awhile, you feel each new financial challenge is a matter of "details, details." You are used to taking money problems in stride, and your tolerant attitude will create the space for more rewarding returns for your efforts to develop.
Dented	Furrowed	The pressures of the last year or more have made you lose confidence in your financial powers. Reassert your vision, rearange your priorities, and raise your "deserve level."
Furrowed	Smooth	After a cycle of hard work to keep afloat under discouraging circumstances, your money prospects are much improved.
Furrowed	Raised	Your patience has brought you to a new turn in the road as you figure out an easier solution to the question of money — and how best to use it.

ND	D	**Financial indications**
Furrowed	Raised/firm	You must feel you have hit the jackpot. What was once hardest to accomplish financially is now a breeze. You must think you are dreaming! But in fact, experience is now on your side.
Furrowed	Raised/soft	Where you see no immediate reward for your efforts to get ahead financially, you often get discouraged. Realize that past problems can be dealt with and resolved with just an extra bit of work.
Furrowed	Dented	You think you are stuck in a cycle where money never materializes as you want it, and the pressure is mounting up. You are about to take charge of all the details that used to overwhelm you and make more of the assets you do have.

ND	**D**	**Financial indications**
Furrowed	Furrowed	You can learn a lot from past obstacles to having a fat bank account. You know the key to success lies in moderation — spend a little, save a little — and do not be afraid to believe in your ability to push ahead to success in money matters soon.

12

Your Relationship Story

To follow the record of the state of your relationships as it is recorded in your ring finger middle knuckle shape, compare the shape of the knuckle on the nondominant hand with the shape of the knuckle on the dominant hand. The contrast in shape reveals how your relationships have developed over the last year or two, and where they are heading, based on current indications.

In the following chart, "ND" means the middle knuckle on the ring finger of the nondominant hand, and "D" refers to the middle knuckle on the ring finger of the dominant hand.

ND	D	Relationship indications
Smooth	Smooth	You have listened to your heart, and the love you have for others is returned to you. You offer support to others because you feel secure. Your love life continues smoothly.
Smooth	Raised	Your experience with others has taught you that people can be trusted to be their best with encouragement and a chance to grow. Your view on love is progressive and your relationships are solid.
Smooth	Raised/firm	Your belief in fate and openness to people around you has led you to become involved in many unusual situations. The returns you get for your interest and participation in relationships are enormous. Get set to welcome more people into your life.

ND	D	Relationship indications
Smooth	Raised/soft	You have always believed in others. Now your faith is being tested. You wait patiently for the issues of another's path to become clear, so that you can build for the future.
Smooth	Dented	Relationships have brought you happiness and peace in the past. This secure foundation in love will see you through present pressures in your dealings with others. You are appreciated by a special person.
Smooth	Furrowed	The happiness you have known in love taught you the ways of the human heart. Hold on to this knowledge as you take on a new challenge in your relationships. Be open to receiving love yourself.

ND	**D**	**Relationship indications**
Raised	Smooth	Early in life you knew that you had to be involved with others to be a complete and happy person. You worked hard at relating to others, and now have a chance for real happiness. The door to good communication is open.
Raised	Raised	You sing the praises of others, and your willingness to give anyone a boost or a smile creates an atmosphere where relationships flourish. Your past successes are your key to the future.
Raised	Raised/firm	You have always felt the need for people, joining clubs, accepting role models. Your admiration and respect for others is the map to your current prospects for love. Go for it!

ND	D	Relationship indications
Raised	Raised/soft	Always cheerful in your past outlook on love, you now wonder why another person seems to be indifferent or in a tight spot. Patience and understanding will work wonders for your current needs.
Raised	Dented	You love people and your good skills in dealing with them help you create a base of understanding at a difficult turning point. Past experience lets you know what you will and won't accept in relationships now.
Raised	Furrowed	Sitting, waiting, sitting and waiting some more isn't really your style. In the past you have been active, and that makes today's restricted circumstances harder to accept. So change what you can, and establish a new direction in your relationships.

ND	D	Relationship indications
Raised/firm	Smooth	You are pleased to meet new people. Your affections are large enough to include family and friends, even strangers who need your help. A humanitarian spirit eases your way in the world and at home. Past experience sets you up for a happy future.
Raised/firm	Raised	The excellence which marks the relationships you create comes from the willingness to put yourself on the line. You are willing to take risks in love. Nothing ventured, nothing gained.
Raised/firm	Raised/firm	Dynamic and loving, you concentrate energy on family and friends, hoping to create a better world. Your past has taught you the value of people, of understanding and encouraging their dreams. You prefer an active role in the world. Others learn from you.

ND	D	Relationship indications
Raised/firm	Raised/soft	It's a mad, mad world! People in your life have been cooperative and loving; when you find an exception to this happy state of being, you wonder where you went wrong. Most likely, you didn't. Know you are in a cycle requiring patience in relationships.
Raised/firm	Dented	From the heights to the depths! Love is a roller coaster. Your past security is now jarred by a new event in your love life. You will cope, using all you know to increase your chances to have and keep your happiness.
Raised/firm	Furrowed	That sinking feeling! Is it love or a charade? Relationships have seemed to develop in a fog lately. But at least the rose-colored glasses are off. Reconsider situations in light of new facts. Clear goals give a new sense of peace.

ND	D	Relationship indications
Raised/soft	Smooth	When you have been discouraged in love in the past, you have been patient and continued to care. You now have the satisfaction of knowing you did your best under less than ideal circumstances, and now the coast is clear. Rebirth in love follows.
Raised/soft	Raised	When love at times in the past has been "a pain," you have hung in there. Little known to you, you were absorbing details about the dynamics of love that have now inspired you to take a more positive, confident approach. Relationships can now satisfy your expectations.

ND	D	Relationship indications
Raised/soft	Raised/firm	Emotions once threatened to overwhelm you and you nearly gave up on love. Today you are glad you didn't join a monastery, as love is exciting. You have earned satisfaction and will take care to hold on to what you have and guard the ones you love.
Raised/soft	Raised/soft	You feel your loves are "karmic." A designated soul mate can be more trouble that it's worth. Concentrate on the here and now, appreciate the ordinary path of love, the highs and lows, and most of all, its enduring quality. Time is on your side.

ND	D	Relationship indications
Raised/soft	Dented	"Singing the blues" makes you feel better. Past experience has taught you it's better to express what's on your mind, not to hide your feelings in hopes a challenge to your affections will go away on its own. Current pressures force you to take the upper hand. Asserting yourself helps your relationships grow, much to your surprise.
Raised/soft	Furrowed	"Simply living a lie." That refrain means, in this case, that you are not claiming the attention and respect you deserve. When you put too much of yourself into a situation without adequate returns, you feel low. You are now able to work at a relationship without putting so much emphasis on sheer endurance. You want more; setting out to get it validates your worth and happiness.

ND	D	Relationship indications
Dented	Smooth	Last year may not have been the most rewarding year for you in matters of the heart, with pressures in many of your relationships. But now your love life can proceed smoothly.
Dented	Raised	Last year's problem is this year's miracle. Now you can believe in the healing power of others' concerns, and gain a foothold on your romantic path. Love is full of possibilities.
Dented	Raised/firm	Relief! You tried so hard in the past, juggling time and energy to make your relationships perfect — you didn't realize how much you would shortly have to show for your efforts. You have reason to be thrilled. Life looks good.

ND	D	Relationship indications
Dented	Raised/soft	Where you were focused on specific needs last year, you now find the whole game of love a bit disconcerting. The best approach is to find a new way to express yourself in love, letting pride in your choices show. This is not the time to be humble.
Dented	Dented	You could easily throw your hands in the air and say "I quit!" Go ahead. Rebel. On your own terms, set guidelines for healthy and rewarding love situations. Experience has taught you that you must say no to unreasonable pressures.
Dented	Furrowed	Rushing into love without brakes for your wilder expectations has taught you to look twice at any situation; get a grip on the ins and outs, choosing your risks. Look hard at how appreciated you and your efforts are.

ND	D	Relationship indications
Furrowed	Smooth	A winter of discontent has thawed into a prospect for happiness in love. Reward those who have stuck by you with a token of thanks.
Furrowed	Raised	You've seen the best and the worst in love. You felt stuck in a situation, and with insight and inspiration, regained the freedom to be yourself. Now you can give more to others and get more in return.
Furrowed	Raised/firm	"When you wish upon a star ..." When love was a drag, you never lost sight of happier times and the belief they would return. Now you have a shot at double the happiness. Love blossoms.
Furrowed	Raised/soft	When you felt unappreciated, people could show you how much you meant when you least expected it. Take the quirks of human nature less seriously and welcome a new cycle of expectations.

ND	D	Relationship indications
Furrowed	Dented	A shift in expectations for the future has brought clarity on issues and a new determination to "get it right." You are surrounded by opportunities, even though the pressure is enormous. Prepare for a welcome change in your emotional life.
Furrowed	Furrowed	Sometimes you think you are on a slow boat to China, not the Love Boat! You're right, if you think Mother Nature, or someone in the flesh, has conspired to teach you the patience of a saint. Your halo glows — now spread some of that love and care into the cultivation of your own dreams.

13 Your Ability to Negotiate

To follow the record of your ability to negotiate as it is recorded in your little finger middle knuckle shape, compare the shape of the knuckle on the nondominant hand with the shape of the knuckle on the dominant hand. The contrast in shape reveals how your ability to negotiate has developed over the last year or two, and where your skills are heading, based on current indications.

In the following chart, "ND" means the middle knuckle on the little finger of the nondominant hand, and "D" refers to the middle knuckle on the little finger of the dominant hand.

ND	D	**Negotiation ability**
Smooth	Smooth	Your realistic and reasonable approach works. You know how to say the right thing to make others comfortable. Your negotiation skills have paved the way for new opportunities, the spin-offs of previous success. Check them out now.
Smooth	Raised	Your past negotiation skills have produced such feedback that now you are encouraged to take on a complicated project that could pay you handsomely. Leave no stone unturned in pursuing your newest goal. You are lucky.
Smooth	Raised/firm	You often suspect you have a charmed life. It's in the people you know and the flow of opportunity. You rarely ignore any encouraging signals from others. You can sell ideas easily now, because you have acquired skills and interests that attract others.

ND	D	**Negotiation ability**
Smooth	Raised/soft	You have kept on top of challenging develop-ments in your projects and nipped opposition in the bud. Now that circumstances seem to call for vigorous action, you have to seize the moment. Courage leads you to your goal.
Smooth	Dented	You could count on a return for your effort in the past, knowing oth-ers respond well to you. An event may not catch you off guard. Call on friends for assistance. Research any thorny issue and take action, and you will come out ahead.
Smooth	Furrowed	When a productive cycle of effort and achievement gets bogged down, take a break from hard work. If you are blocked in the design of your life, take a new look at what matters to you. Desires can change without conscious awareness. A review of priorities is in order now.

ND	D	**Negotiation ability**
Raised	Smooth	You have had great results in the past when you worked hard to push your projects and plans through to completion. Your planning ability now continues to point you in the right direction — to your goals!
Raised	Raised	Pssst — wanna make a deal? You know how to put ideas out there at just the right moment to just the right person. Keep talking. Your past success now leads to further gains.
Raised	Raised/firm	Your track record gives evidence of a flair for negotiations, a vision that takes your dealings and goals out of the ordinary. Use your past achievements as stepping stones to a bright future. Others are willing to help you carry out your dreams.

ND	D	Negotiation ability
Raised	Raised/soft	You know you have accomplished a lot in the past few years. Do not "hide your light under a bushel basket" now, or take shelter in the shadow of others' achievements. You can win out over present challenging circumstances.
Raised	Dented	Aren't you glad you've achieved so many of your goals? You have proven you can do what you set your mind to — now get going on the current problem and show the world you haven't lost your touch.
Raised	Furrowed	A past cycle of success has probably put you on the map. Because you gave the competition a run for its money, the competition is now after you. Remember, you love a challenge — opposition gets you going.

ND	**D**	**Negotiation ability**
Raised/firm	Smooth	After an ambitious cycle of achievement, with many irons in the fire, you are ready to sit a minute and survey the territory you have created. Decide what you like best in all your options and choose a new plan of attack. Luck is on your side.
Raised/firm	Raised	A high profile in your community or among your peers gives you the reputation as the can-do person you are. Think about new territory or skills you want to acquire now. With these in place, you will increase the guarantee of accomplishment.
Raised/firm	Raised/firm	Confidence and a driving ambition lead you to take on challenges, just to prove you can succeed against the odds. Empires are built by people like you. Expand your interests now because you're on a roll. "Time and tide wait for no man."

ND	**D**	**Negotiation ability**
Raised/firm	Raised/soft	You thought reputation and success would always keep you out of "harm's way." Troubled waters mean people or circumstances you must get around to re-establish your control and magic touch. Simplify your approach. You can succeed.
Raised/firm	Dented	Current annoyances don't reflect past certainties. You know the rules which work for you. Use them now to assert your values and win out over pressures. Try a different angle as you pursue your aims.
Raised/firm	Furrowed	Disappointment currently blasts your normally tranquil cycle of achievement. You have accidentally overloaded your schedule to the point where you feel a bit overwhelmed. Go back to the beginning; remember that adrenaline rush small opportunities used to give.

ND	D	**Negotiation ability**
Raised/soft	Smooth	In the past, you haven't gotten your projects done as quickly as you would like. Either circumstances were against it or you were likely to procrastinate. All that has changed now in a new cycle of success on the horizon.
Raised/soft	Raised	Ambivalence about your goals and your best options in the past kept you from steady achievement. Now success has sharpened your vision and your aims are clearly in focus. You will achieve much.
Raised/soft	Raised/firm	Those who served as sounding boards for your projects once let you down, and you went through a period of distrusting all but your own judgment. Today you have able and talented people to consult who will advance your cause.

ND	D	**Negotiation ability**
Raised/soft	Raised/soft	Signals that you haven't been on the right course have been coming at you for some time. Now is the moment to look at that fork in the road and go for a new adventure. Changing your tactics brings success.
Raised/soft	Dented	You have been patient for awhile as developments in your life were not what you expected. You have patience and a thoughtful approach on your side. You can now outwit the opposition. A challenge stirs you to new action.
Raised/soft	Furrowed	You thought you had to swallow your pride and accept circumstances that failed to meet your standards. Now you see clearly you must ask for more — or start over on your own. Honor your independence.

ND	D	**Negotiation ability**
Dented	Smooth	Previous pressures have lifted. In the last year you learned a valuable lesson in communication. People don't always hear what is said. You have learned to make your point more forcefully, and can now achieve your goals.
Dented	Raised	Last year, life on the fast track had its rewards and pitfalls. You now take the essence of what you learned last year — about people, their needs, and their response to you — and forge ahead with renewed strength.
Dented	Raised/firm	Timing is everything! You have used last year's challenges and irritations to set new goals for yourself. You can push through all your newest ideas. Your confidence and "all systems go" attitude makes for rapid advancement.

ND	**D**	**Negotiation ability**
Dented	Raised/soft	You wish others could understand the pressures that led you to today's discouraging state of affairs. You can now clear up that project dearest to your heart, and succeed by eliminating non-essentials. Do not be distracted.
Dented	Dented	Unlikely events are the catalyst to a new life. Last year taught you to be prepared for anything as you put your life in order and established a solid, satisfying lifestyle. After you straighten out one more issue, you can relax and regroup.
Dented	Furrowed	Don't let the issues from the past year get away from you now. You can straighten out the conflicts still asking for your attention. This year's prospects are preferable. You have only to take a firm stance to insure a more tranquil life.

ND	D	Negotiation ability
Furrowed	Smooth	A past cycle of delay and frustration has taught you to push forward whenever possible. Your improved sense of timing eases your path now. You will welcome new opportunities and the open doors that greet you.
Furrowed	Raised	At last! No more nonsense! The people in the past who have not seemed serious about their participation in your plans are now ready to work. Circumstances are much more favorable.
Furrowed	Raised/firm	Not so long ago you wondered what it would take to get your plans on target. A miracle, maybe. Your vision was out of sync with the exact options then available. You persisted. Now the world is ready for your ideas, and options you only dreamed of are now a reality.

ND	**D**	**Negotiation ability**
Furrowed	Raised/soft	You have been patient with people and circumstances, and with gains that are slow to materialize. Choose new goals and communicate desires clearly. With a new focus, your projects fall into place more quickly.
Furrowed	Dented	Old delays that made you feel stuck have crystallized into issues you are in a position to do something about. Growing pressures have helped you realize what you need to do to ensure the success of your projects.
Furrowed	Furrowed	You deserve a change of scene. Scrap old projects that hang over your head and have little chance of working out. Pick two or three close friends, people you trust, to help you clear out the deadwood and open the gate to the magical future you now suspect can be a reality.

COMPARING THE FIRMNESS
OF MOUNTS AND KNUCKLES

The shape of the knuckles reveals the potential for success for each area of life that the fingers represent. As we just saw, a smooth or raised knuckle, especially if it is firm, represents success-in-the-making, while a dented, furrowed, or soft raised ridge signals challenges to potential success.

On the palm side of the hand, the mounts are evaluated in exactly the same way. The shape of each mount defines potential and talent in the area of life that the mount represents. To be a good mount, a mount has to be high (raised) and preferably firm. This indicates that the person is using the potential the mount represents. If the qualities for potential success are not being used, a mount is flat or soft. This is the same as a soft raised ridge or a dent or furrow, which shows similar obstacles and challenges.

If you wonder why a soft raised ridge is so different in meaning from a raised ridge, just think of the difference between a soft or firm mount on the palm. The principle is the same.

The firmness of the area is the clue to actively used potential. A smooth knuckle, with no raised ridges, is always firm to the touch because the skin lies close to the bone and cartilage underneath. This is why a smooth knuckle has a positive meaning.

The difference between mount shape and knuckle shape is that the knuckles record in more graphic detail our past experience and its influence on us. With this past as a guideline, we have a picture of how the future will develop and when.

The knuckles can be timed in a way that mounts cannot, because there are four sets of knuckles on the fingers, which are the active, conscious area of the hand.

With the mounts and knuckles, we are monitoring two different areas of an individual's life. The mounts are a guide to a person's energy, and the knuckles are a guide to conditions that affect that energy.

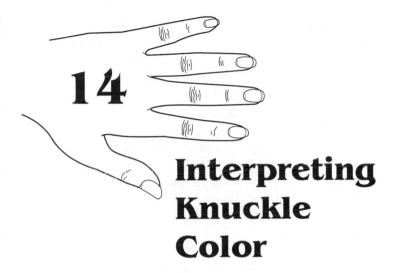

Interpreting Knuckle Color

Color in the knuckles is nearly a magical phenomenon in the way it gives clues to the future. With color, we come to the heart of what many people find fascinating about palmistry — its ability to make predictions. Of course, all aspects of the palm and the back of the hand lend themselves to the predictive art, but none so instantly or in such a simple manner as color.

We learned in Chapter 8 that color in the knuckles works just like color does in a face. A person will blush or become pale with a certain stimulus, and the color change reveals an inner state or emotion. A knuckle will become more pink or more pale with the inner but unconscious knowledge of the short-term future. In either case, the blood vessels either expand or contract in response to a stimulus.

In the case of a face, the stimulus has already happened at the moment the face changes color. Color in the knuckles is a bit different, for while color in a face is a response to something that has happened and is a fact, color in the knuckles can come as a result of a fact — the future — which is not yet here.

The best way to understand how features in knuckles work is to compare them to the features of a face. We just studied shape in the knuckles and the way that shape expresses our conditioning as a result of experience. Our experience helps shape our future.

Think for a moment of the art of reading facial features. A certain shape of nose or forehead or eyebrow can be used to make statements about a person's character, and what he or she is likely to do based on that character. The shape of a face is a long-term indicator of behavior or type, and the future that grows out of it.

Shape in the knuckles is very similar. That shape can change, slowly, over a period of time. Knuckle shape is a reliable long-term indicator of what a person is likely to do, based on the conditioning experience has provided.

Now think of expressions on a face and how quickly they can come and go. Expressions can be fleeting or habitual, depending on the stimulus. The face has the ability to express the life force as it filters through.

Color in the knuckles is another expression of the life force and how this force affects our future. Because the essence of life is change — new opportunities arise, old ones fall away; parts of our lives are successful and complete, others are not yet successful or are incomplete — the color in the knuckles has the ability to change also, to reflect the different aspects of our lives. Color in the knuckles is a short-term indicator of current reality as it affects us now and will affect us in the future.

To understand the difference between shape and color in a knuckle, realize that shape is based on something that has already happened, a given, much as the shape of a face is a given; color is like an expression, an indicator of life potential in the here and now, that influences the present and the future. That is why color is a good indicator of what's happening in our lives.

To use the colors effectively, we have to apply their meaning to each set of knuckles and to each finger, but the first step to working with color in the knuckles is to know what colors to look for and what they mean.

Skin tone	**Color variations**
White or light skin	The average skin tone which matches the overall skin color.
	A degree of pink, which is a plus, or surplus of color.
	A pale tone, which is a minus, or absence of color.

Skin tone	Color variations
Olive or tan skin	The average skin tone which matches the overall skin color.
	A contrasting degree of pink, but usually less than on light skin.
	A paler tone, noticeably lighter than the original skin tone, but not as pale as it is on light skin.
Brown or black skin	(Here the pink and pale contrasts do not apply. Other indicators work as well as the pink and white contrasts on lighter skin.)
	The average skin tone which matches the overall skin color.
	A noticeably shiny area covering part of the knuckle works the same way as pink.
	A duller patch of skin without the shine, or a darker patch of pigment, as if the color has pooled, works the same as a pale color on light skin.

Whether the skin you are working with is black or white or in between, a little practice will easily reveal that every knuckle has contrasting shades of color on it.

Color variations are more noticeable on some knuckles than on others, so it is important to look at a number of hands to get used to seeing the color differences. On some light hands, the pink color, on either the middle or tip knuckles, can approach a reddish shade. On other light hands, the pink is faint, just a blush or hint of increased color. Learning to spot these differences will gradually alert you to the fact that the intensity of color does matter. The greater the contrasts, the greater the significance.

THE MEANING OF THE COLORS

Pink is always the color that states, "Something's happening, things are moving along." The same is true for a shine on black skin. White or pale colors always tell us, "Something's slowed down here. Nothing much is moving along." The same is true for dull or dark patches on dark-skinned knuckles.

A very pink color, verging on red, means, "Things are happening fast, hold on to your hat!" The same is true for very shiny skin on dark knuckles. And a very pale color means, "Whoa, we are really stuck here. There's no future here." The same is true for very dull or dark patches of skin on a dark knuckle.

To determine what's happening and how fast, we learn to identify the differences in color, or shine, and their contrasts. A slight contrast in color in the knuckle will indicate a moderately-paced change in a life; a great difference in contrast in the knuckle's color will mean a rapid change in that life.

The fun of reading color in knuckles is looking for the pink or shine, to be able to predict an event or an outcome to a situation that is under scrutiny. Because pink or shine in a knuckle shows what's happening, those shades make it possible to predict an event. Because an absence of color or shine means nothing's happening, those shades imply that an event or situation will not develop.

To summarize the colors' meanings, pink means a positive momentum, while white means a negative momentum.

To explain further, pink shows a heightened energy that makes things happen. That heightened energy is a combination of what the world brings and how the person responds to the world. White, with a negative momentum, is not a signal of a negative event, but simply of slower or absent movement toward a goal. A white color means the world will not present an opportunity, or the person will not make use of what the world offers. In any case, something always materializes out of a pink color, and nothing materializes out of a pale color. The above explanation of momentum applies equally to a shine or lack of shine on dark skin.

These are the principles of energy that accompany the colors. According to these principles, color can be applied to the knuckles as a whole, to each set of knuckles, and to each individual finger.

Noting the color on the knuckles as a whole is a quick way to determine if a person's life is now action-packed or more relaxed, in general. Analyzing the color on each set of knuckles gives an idea of where the key to success or challenges lies, and the timing for this success or these challenges. To understand where success or challenges are focused, use the meaning of each separate finger.

Overall color	Meaning
All knuckles pink (shiny on dark skin)	Life is on an upswing now. Anything can happen, and good news comes in bunches. Opportunity and success abound.
All knuckles pale (dull or darker on dark skin)	Not much is happening right now. Examine your life to see where you can create activity. Visualize what use you can make of the past and present to get ahead in the future.

To understand the meaning of color on the four sets of knuckles, let's review the location of each set of knuckles, and the timing for them.

Set	Location	Time Frame
1	ND middle	One or more years in the past; up to 3 years in the future
2	ND tip	6 months in the past; up to 3 years in the future

Set	Location	Time Frame
3	D middle	Present time, 4-month span: 2 months ahead, 2 months behind
4	D tip	6–18 months ahead

Now let's review the names and meaning of the four sets of knuckles.

Set	Name	Meaning
1	Background knuckles	Refer to the accumulation of our past experience and how it affects our future.
2	Catalyst knuckles	Reveal details about people, places, and events over the last 6 months which will affect our future.
3	Present knuckles	Describe circumstances, people, and places that currently affect our future.

Set	Name	Meaning
4	Future knuckles	Focus on events, people, and places that will affect our future in the next 6 to 18 months.

Using these sets of knuckles, we can get a preview of what, out of our present and past opportunities, will pan out for the future, and help us reach our goals.

INTERPRETING COLOR

Set	Color	Meaning
1	Pink/shiny	The people you have met and the activites you have participated in through the last year will be a help in the future.

Set	Color	Meaning
1	Pale/dull	The people you have met and the activites you have participated in through the last year are not the key to your future success. Look for new situations.
2	Pink/shiny	People, places, and events in the last 6 months are an important part of your future and can lead to success.
2	Pale/dull	People, places and events of the last 6 months are not a key to your future.
3	Pink/shiny	Your present circumstances are helpful. Expect success now for your projects.

Set	Color	Meaning
3	Pale/dull	Your present circumstances are not the key to success. See how you can smooth the way with a different approach.
4	Pink/shiny	The next 6 to 18 months hold many rewards for you.
4	Pale/dull	The next 6 to 18 months are not the essential key to your success. Revise your plans as best you can to attract success.

This chart will help you distinguish the time frames and stimulus for success that each set of knuckles can reveal. What you must remember about a pink or shiny skin tone is that it means live potential. When you review the time frames for each set of knuckles, you are only describing when and how potential becomes alive: from your long-term past (set 1), from the short-term past (set 2), from the present (set 3), or as a result of the immediate future (set 4).

EXAMPLES OF THE MESSAGE OF COLOR

Let's say that your first set of knuckles are pink. Great! This means that what you have experienced in the last year or more will lead to success in the future. When in the future will your ship come in? You will have to check the knuckles on the dominant hand, the present and future knuckles, to answer that question.

If your good luck is arriving now, the middle knuckles will be pink. If your good fortune is expected in six to eighteen months, then the tip knuckles on the dominant hand will be pink or shiny.

Next, think about this case: Your first set of knuckles are pink, and no other set of knuckles is pink. Not the present knuckles, not the future knuckles. What now? What happened to your fortune? The answer is that the good luck and success promised by the pink on your first set of knuckles is coming – but further ahead than eighteen months. At this point, you have to remind yourself that the future represented by the knuckles on the nondominant hand goes up to three years ahead. And, if only the knuckles on the nondominant hand are pink, then the promise is for later than the extension in time (one and a half years) found on the dominant hand. That is, your success will arrive anywhere from one and a half to three years in the future.

But, be assured that wherever a pink color is found on a knuckle, good luck, success, and fulfillment follow.

Many times, we will have a question about just one area of our life which concerns us most. At this point, we can check the finger related to that area for a quick answer to how things will turn out.

Let's review the meanings of the fingers: the index finger relates to your career, the middle finger to your finances, the ring finger to your relationships, and the little figure to your ability to negotiate.

Now let's apply the color interpretations to each finger, knuckle by knuckle, to help you be more specific in your ability to decode the finger and knuckle meanings.

Finger	Hand	Knuckle	Color	Meaning
Index	ND	Middle	Pink	Your career is helped along by people and circumstances in your life a year or more ago.
Index	ND	Middle	Pale	Circumstances from a year or more ago are not especially helpful to your career over the next several years.
Index	ND	Tip	Pink	People and circumstances from the last 6 months help advance your career.

Finger	Hand	Knuckle	Color	Meaning
Index	ND	Tip	Pale	People and circumstances from the last 6 months are not especially helpful to your career.
Index	D	Middle	Pink	Great things are happening in your career now. You could be promoted.
Index	D	Middle	Pale	Your work life is a little sluggish. Present circumstances should not be viewed as a stepping stone to success.
Index	D	Tip	Pink	The next 6 to 18 months promise rewards in your career.
Index	D	Tip	Pale	The next 6 to 18 months are not the key to future success. Work now to create new opportunities.

Finger	Hand	Knuckle	Color	Meaning
Middle	ND	Middle	Pink	All your activities and contacts from a year or more ago will be financially rewarding in your future.
Middle	ND	Middle	Pale	Activities and contacts from a year or more ago are not the key to future financial success.
Middle	ND	Tip	Pink	People, places, and events from the last 6 months will pay off, bringing financial rewards.
Middle	ND	Tip	Pale	The last 6 months are not the key to future success.
Middle	D	Middle	Pink	Present opportunities to make money pay off. You may get a bonus or a raise. Now is a good time to buy or sell.

Finger	Hand	Knuckle	Color	Meaning
Middle	D	Middle	Pale	Don't look for any payoff from present opportunities. Now is not the time to buy or sell.
Middle	D	Tip	Pink	The next 6 to 18 months will be financially rewarding.
Middle	D	Tip	Pale	No great financial gains can be expected in the next 6 to 18 months.
Ring	ND	Middle	Pink	Your relationships in the last year or more ago lead to happiness and fulfillment in the future. If you met someone during this time, the relationship can work well.

Finger	Hand	Knuckle	Color	Meaning
Ring	ND	Middle	Pale	Your relationships in the last year or more ago are not the key to future happiness. Work to improve existing relationships. This includes family and close friends as well as lovers.
Ring	ND	Tip	Pink	People and circumstances in the last 6 months contribute to your future happiness. Relationships begun or continued during this time will be successful in the near future.
Ring	ND	Tip	Pale	Love in the last 6 months has not been the optimum experience for your near future happiness.

Finger	Hand	Knuckle	Color	Meaning
Ring	D	Middle	Pink	Relationships are going well now. If you are not attached to anyone, you could meet a special person during the next 2 months.
Ring	D	Middle	Pale	Relationships now are not all you could hope for. Look for ways to improve existing relationships.
Ring	D	Tip	Pink	The next 6 to 18 months ahead are happy times for your relationships.
Ring	D	Tip	Pale	The next 6 to 18 months are a time for work and growth in your relationships.
Little	ND	Middle	Pink	Your negotiations in the last year or more ago lead to success in the future.

Finger	Hand	Knuckle	Color	Meaning
Little	ND	Middle	Pale	Your negotiations over the last year or more ago are not the key to future success. Set new terms and goals now.
Little	ND	Tip	Pink	Negotiations in the last 6 months are a key to future success. You have chosen the right projects to be involved with.
Little	ND	Tip	Pale	Projects and goals from the last 6 months need to be revised to gather the success you expect.
Little	D	Middle	Pink	You have great ability to negotiate right now for your goals.
Little	D	Middle	Pale	Rethink your present projects. Look to other outlets for success now.

Finger	Hand	Knuckle	Color	Meaning
Little	D	Tip	Pink	The next 6 to 18 months are very favorable. You can achieve many of your goals and dreams.
Little	D	Tip	Pale	Add to efforts at success, and you can stir up opportunities that are not predicted for the next 6 to 18 months. Success will take work.

With these charts you have the keys for interpreting color in the knuckles in general, in sets, and on each finger. As you can see, the meaning is modified by the hand and knuckle involved. Color matters in every knuckle.

Practice reading at least a dozen sets of knuckles and you will see that you quickly get the hang of it. For now, we are only concerned with pink or pale tones; that is, with an increase or decrease in color as a signal of increased or decreased momentum in the areas of life that the hands, fingers, and knuckles represent.

In the next chapter, we are going to refine our use of color and learn another of its amazing properties as a vehicle for prediction.

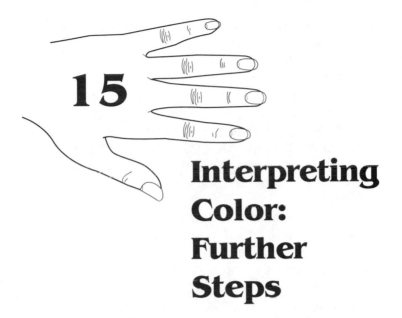

15

Interpreting Color: Further Steps

Color in the knuckles is a more versatile feature than anyone might imagine at first glance. A quick look at any knuckle will reveal that different shades of color coexist in the knuckle. One area on a knuckle will have average skin tone appropriate to the person's overall coloring; another part of the knuckle will appear to be pink or shiny, or dull and pale, compared to the basic skin tone.

In the last chapter, we learned the meaning for these basic color differences, and how to apply them to the knuckles as a whole. In this chapter we are going to learn how to apply the meaning of color to the knuckles in separate parts.

For instance, you can check any knuckle to verify that pink occurs on any part of that knuckle, and know that pink means something good is happening in the time frame the knuckle indicates and in the area of life the finger represents. As an example, pink anywhere on the middle knuckle of the index finger on the dominant hand means a person's career is progressing very well right now.

As another example, you find you have some pink on the tip knuckle of the middle finger of your nondominant hand. This means, in general, that activities from the last six months will pay off in the near future.

Suppose you wanted more specific information. Who, among all your contacts from the last six months, will be most helpful? And where are the opportunities you have created in the last six months going to show up? This is where the tendency of color to cover only part of a knuckle comes in handy. Each little area within the knuckle has its own private meaning.

To understand this, think a minute about the whole surface of a palm, and the fact that the palm is divided into mounts, each of which has its own meaning. Heightened color can exist in just one mount, highlighting its meaning at the time of interpretation.

The same thing happens on the knuckles. Only part of a knuckle will be pink or pale, giving meaning to that part alone.

Here we are going to divide the knuckle first into two zones. In Chapter 2, we had a quick look at the traditional three zones of the hand, created by horizontal divisions of the palm. (For another reference to zones and their interpretation, see *Palmistry, The Whole View*, Chapter 10, Llewellyn

Publications.) The concept of zones in palmistry is a standard one.

Those of you who are already familiar with palmistry may know that a vertical line drawn down the center of the middle finger and the palm divides the palm into two zones: the conscious half and the unconscious half.

The thumb side of the palm represents the conscious zone, and the little finger side of the palm reflects the unconscious zone. This principle works exactly the same on the fingers, seen from the back of the hand. The half facing the thumb, on any finger, represents the conscious zone; the half facing the little finger, on any finger, reflects the unconscious zone.

We'll call these zones 1 and 2. Zone 1 belongs to the thumb side and conscious half of the finger; zone 2 to the little finger side and unconscious half of the finger.

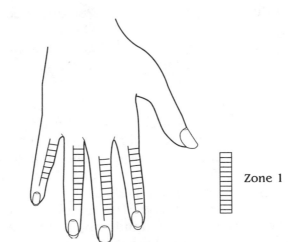

Zone 1 will represent personal skills and conditions under an individual's control, because it represents the conscious zone. Zone 2 will refer to conditions larger than the individual, conditions that are beyond personal control, as this zone represents the unconscious.

Here is a chart to summarize the meaning of the zones on each finger.

Finger	Zone	Meaning
Index	1	Personal work skills
Index	2	The management or owners of the company
Middle	1	Personal financial skills
Middle	2	The economy
Ring	1	Personal relationship skills
Ring	2	Others' relationship skills as they affect you
Little	1	Personal negotiating skills
Little	2	Others' negotiating skills as they affect you

Learning this division of the length of the fingers into two zones is the first step to applying color in concentrated areas. Using this system, you can look for color on just one half or the other. Zone 1 refers to your working, financial, relationship, or negotiating skills. Zone 2 refers to conditions that affect you. This is another example of the worlds of the hand, applied on a miniature basis, useful for describing a situation in greater detail.

Pink Color

Finger	Zone	Meaning
Index	1	Your work skills are in peak form. You can be sure you are doing your job well, and will advance.
Index	2	The prospects for the company you work for are good. It is worth your time to be there.
Middle	1	Your financial prospects are excellent. Be alert to new ways to make money. You may receive a raise.
Middle	2	The economy affects you positively. The marketplace you are concerned with will produce for you.
Ring	1	You are hot! Be secure in the knowledge that you are handling relationships well.
Ring	2	Others are a positive influence on you. Your relationships should be pleasant.
Little	1	Your negotiating skills are great. Communications go well, and you get ahead.

Finger	Zone	Meaning
Little	2	Others' desires and projects affect you positively. Be alert for opportunity.

PALE COLOR

Finger	Zone	Meaning
Index	1	Your work skills are not up to the demands of the situation. Brush up and increase your learning curve.
Index	2	The management of your company is ineffective. This sign often occurs during transition periods, such as mergers. If you own your own company, read zone 2 as market conditions, not the owner. When you are the owner, your personal skills are found in zone 1. If you are the owner and this section is pale, then market conditions operate against you at this time.
Middle	1	Your financial conditions need improving. Read up on new ways to make money and to make it work for you.

Finger	Zone	Meaning
Middle	2	The economy as it affects you is sluggish. Take precautions to guard what you have already earned.
Ring	1	You are feeling a little low in the relationship department. Raise your expectations, and try harder.
Ring	2	Others don't quite understand you. See that you get the credit you deserve — nicely. Talk to others, if possible, to improve communications.
Little	1	Your negotiating skills need polishing. Be confident of the rewards for your skills and interests.
Little	2	Others are not communicating clearly with you. Ask direct questions, but be tactful.

Looking at color in these two zones of the knuckles, you have a clue to the source of your success and who is going to play a role in it: yourself or others. You can measure the relative strength of your own efforts, seen in zone 1, and the amount of support given to you by others or outside sources, seen in zone 2.

Color has a further role to play when we begin our study of the warrior figures in the knuckles. These figures help us identify people who play a role in our lives, and if that role is active, a pink color will surround those figures. We will shortly learn more about who matters in our lives in our search for success.

Now we come to one of the most exciting and unusual uses of color in the knuckles — make it a way to determine *where* our success is likely to be found.

The knuckles can be divided into another set of zones, into the four directions of the compass: north, south, east, and west. Directions in the knuckles are shown below to the left.

Using these areas of the knuckles as a guide to success, we can note which sections are pink, and those are the areas that lead to our success.

A boundary of these four directions is necessary if we are going to be more specific. It isn't realistic to assume that, for instance, because the south part of the knuckle is pink that our success could come from anywhere in the entire world that is considered south.

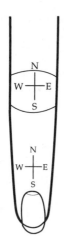

To keep our analysis simple, the boundaries for the four directions will be the same as the country in which the person lives. For all United States citizens, we view the knuckle as if it were a map of the United States. For someone living in Great Britain, the knuckle is viewed as a map of Great Britain. This statement holds true of any country in the world where the person who is having his or her knuckles analyzed lives. The boundaries are the same as the country in which the person lives.

Using the four directions and the map of the country the person lives in, you can be as general or as specific as you like when you analyze the best locations for opportunity.

You can use just the directions, and keep the analysis short and simple: if the south part of the knuckle is pink or shiny, it is true that somewhere in the whole southern United States (or applicable country) there lies a chance at success. Pink in the south is shown at the right.

You can be slightly more specific using directions alone: not just the south, north, east, or west, but by quadrants, such as the northeast, or the northwest; the southeast, or the southwest.

Now, for the fun part. Suppose you were to superimpose a map on the knuckles, in your mind's eye, and were aware of approximately where Miami, San Francisco, or St. Louis would be located. You could look for pink in those smaller spots on the knuckle, and if you find it, you can predict success from any city that is covered by pink. That is, from any city that would be there if the knuckle were a map of the United States.

To get a feel for this, it is suggested you look at a map of the United States to review just where the major cities are located.

Using these few cities alone as a starting point will reassure you that the system works, and perhaps spur you on to want to learn even more locations. Taking the system further, you could become aware of the general location of all the states, so that you could talk in terms of states as you view the isolated pink areas on a knuckle: mentioning Alabama, Minnesota, Nevada, New York, or whatever.

You will prove yourself amazing the minute you can tell other people what city or what state holds good luck for them. Just a bit of practice will cement the locations in your mind as you look at a knuckle and imagine it as a map with major cities or the states.

You can apply this information about location to the areas of life the fingers represent. For instance, if the southern half of your knuckle on the index finger (either one) is pink, then the potential success in the south relates to work; if on the middle finger, then to finances; on the ring finger, to relationships; and on the little finger, to negotiating ability.

You can now locate potential success in any one of the four areas of your life that the fingers represent; you can name a source for the success — your own or others' efforts; you can identify a location for this success, using the color map of the knuckles; and you can specify a time for this success, according to the time frame of the knuckle on which the pink is found.

Each knuckle has its own set of information. A different city might be highlighted on each knuckle. This means success in work will not be found in the same city as love or money or negotiating skills. As mobile as we are today, many of us live our lives spread from city to city. We might work in New York, have roots in Indiana, and a mother who now lives in San Francisco. All these areas will be highlighted in the knuckles, on the appropriate fingers.

Understanding the fascinating impact of the world around us comes through using color, and combining the messages of all the knuckles. We will learn more about how to do this in Chapter 20 when we begin to put all the features of the knuckles together in a sample analysis.

Reading your own knuckles

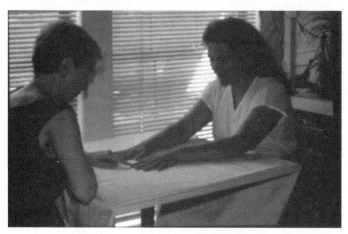

Having your knuckles read

16

Interpreting
Warriors

Most likely warriors have been "hanging out" in knuckles everywhere, unknown to most people, even to the palmists who would be the most interested in them. It is safe to say that from time immemorial and in people of all cultures, knuckles have borne the little images formed by lines that are not as random as they might seem. The images are stark and primitive, resembling folk art.

The ultimate frontier in palmistry in this age is an awareness of the existence of these tiny, unexplored lines in the overlooked area of the knuckles, and the knowledge that these images carry an obvious message. Once it is seen that the small vertical lines in the knuckles form pictures, in hand after hand and finger after finger, we have to conclude that a message is attached to these images. After all, even the lines in the palm have their traditional meanings, and they do not have the advantage of forming a picture that can be easily interpreted according to its form and shape.

The disadvantage of these pictures, we must be quick to note, is that they are so very tiny, and working with them takes skill and patience. But the thrill of discovery and the fun of working with images, something we are very used to experiencing in this day of film and video, quickly makes up for the inconvenience of the small size and relative inaccessibility of the images.

How inaccessible? The images can only be as large as the knuckle itself, and, in many cases, as small as a fraction of the knuckle. And the images appear in an upside down fashion: if the fingers on a hand are extended, pointed outward, the images face away from the person on whose hand they are found.

Another person can see the images on our fingers more easily than we can, due to their upside down position.

The position of the images is quite a commentary in itself. Cooperation with another person is necessary to get the whole picture. The very fact that we need another person to best reveal the images in our knuckles is a testimony to the premise that the back of the hand represents the world around us and the people in it.

It is possible to get a glimpse of the images in your own knuckles. Fold your fingers down over the palm; with the palm facing you, bend your wrist sharply and bring the knuckles up to eye level. This will allow you to get an idea of the warriors and other images, but your wrist and arm stand a chance of tiring before you can adequately take in the whole scene. (See photos on page 212.)

The most comfortable and complete way of looking at these images will be with another person.

Of course, the way the images sit in the knuckles is a plus when you are the one who wants to do the discovering as you look at another person's knuckles. It is very easy and comfortable to look at fingers which are extended toward you. The best way to concentrate is to have the other person put their hands down on a flat surface in a well-lighted area. Daylight is the best light to use when you are first learning to discover these images in the knuckles. Daylight often makes the images come alive and seem to leap out of the knuckles.

The images come in three different types: stick figures, called warriors; fully drawn figures, looking like cartoons; and symbols. In this chapter, we are going to work with the most dynamic and basic image, the warrior.

The centerpiece of all the images in the knuckles is the warrior. This figure is the most simply drawn, the easiest to spot, and expresses most accurately the dynamics of the knuckle's message, that of action in the world and how it affects us. The warriors represent real life people who are connected to us, through whom we experience the world.

The warriors, as we have noted earlier, are stick figures, drawn just as a child would draw an elementary figure, with a circle for a head, a single line for the torso, and the same for the limbs.

This is the most common form for the warrior. The figure can also appear without a circle for a head, having only an extension of the torso as the head of the figure.

At times a warrior can be drawn in an abstract form, rather sketchy-looking, as if it were an asterisk.

No doubt it is best to learn to spot the best drawn form first, the warrior with a head and clearly identifiable limbs, to accustom your eye to the concept. Once you are familiar with that form, you will easily see the abstract ones as well.

You will need to study the posture of the warriors to learn how to interpret them. But before we learn the way to interpret them, let's understand a little more about them.

What are the warriors? Warriors are symbols, actual drawings of a human figure, in a style and posture that looks like a warrior. Their very appearance gives them their name.

What do the warriors do? In the knuckle, warriors are distinguished by their posture. In life, warriors are distinguished by their actions. They go into battle, and they emerge either in victory or in defeat. Warriors in the knuckles imitate this reality, adopting a basic posture of victory or of defeat. These postures will be a signal for the success or lack of a success in a project. To the right is a warrior in a victory posture, and a warrior in a defeated or discouraged posture.

Victorious

In the knuckle, a warrior will also be drawn in postures that reflect its path into battle, in either an aggressive or defensive posture.

A warrior will be drawn in postures that reflect the progress of his battle. He may appear exultant.

Defeated

Or he may be secretive, skulking; standing still; leaping about. It might appear strong or weak.

The variety of postures is enormous, but these attitudes we have just seen are basic to a warrior. The fun of working with warriors is to interpret just what posture is revealed.

Aggressive

How do we use the warriors' information? Just what does a warrior represent, and how do we apply the meaning of the postures? In the knuckle, a warrior represents a person other than oneself. On the index finger, a warrior will represent someone connected to work and career; on the middle finger knuckles, a warrior represents someone connected to our finances; on the ring

Defensive

Exultant

Secretive

Still

Leaping

Strong

Weak

finger, someone we relate to; and on the little finger, someone we negotiate with.

To know how your boss is faring, or a colleague or employee, you may get this information from a warrior in your index finger knuckles. If you are curious about the prosperity or honesty and integrity of your banker, you can learn this from the posture of a warrior in your middle finger knuckles. To see if someone you love — whether a spouse, child, parent, or friend — is happy, you can look at the warriors in your ring finger knuckles. To find out if the other people involved in any project are doing their share and are satisfied with the project, check the warriors in the little finger knuckles.

It is easy to tell a story and predict an outcome to a situation based on the warriors' postures. You will apply the meaning to the area of life represented by the finger where the warrior is found. (Illustrations of the following warriors are on the previous page.)

Victorious posture: Your project will be a success.

Aggressive posture: You are in a strong position to succeed.

Defeated posture: Check to eliminate any potential obstacles to success. As your project is now set up, a successful outcome is in doubt.

Defensive posture: Back off, regroup, and rethink your project. Forces are working against the project.

Exultant posture: You are making excellent progress on the path to success.

Secretive, skulking posture: Hidden factors may threaten the success of your project. Be careful.

Standing still posture: You have reached a plateau in your endeavor. Look to the next steps.

Leaping about posture: Great strides are being made. You can expect success.

Strong posture: There is strength in your projects and plans. Keep on as you are.

Weak posture: You need to bolster your resources, and enlist the aid of strong people for your project.

Practice by looking for only one form on a knuckle, or simply locating any warrior on any knuckle and deciding only if it has a positive or a weak posture. Disregard these categories until you are used to recognizing a strong or a weak warrior in an instant.

ANALYZING WARRIORS

Each part of a warrior's body has a particular significance, for purposes of interpretation.

Head: Represents a person's sense of direction and ability to think clearly.

Torso: Describes the person's fundamental strength or weakness, and sense of purpose in life.

Arms: Represent the ability to stir up action, to make things happen, and to achieve personal aims.

Legs: Represent the solidity of the figure's intentions and ability, as well as a sense of security.

Rules exist to help us understand the warriors' messages. The number one guideline is the study of their posture, which we have just seen. But there are other ways to interpret their messages, too. In addition to posture, there are three ways to analyze warrior figures: by the depth of all their features, the length of their limbs, and the shape of their heads.

Do not begin this analysis until you are very comfortable with your ability to see warriors in the knuckles. After you have seen several, you will gradually become aware of the differences in their limbs and the shapes of their heads.

Depth

The entire warrior figure may not be even in depth. Perhaps the head is drawn more lightly than the torso, or the torso is drawn more lightly than the head. Perhaps one of the arms is drawn more deeply than the other, and the same with the legs. These differences in depth tell us something about the warrior, and by extension, about the person the warrior represents.

Deeply drawn lines, as a rule, are positive, a sign of strength and certainty. Lightly drawn lines are less positive, a relative sign of weakness and confusion.

To apply this, look carefully at the warrior you have spotted. Are all the components of the figure — the head, the torso, the arms and legs — the same depth? Or is one feature drawn more lightly than the rest, or more deeply? Typically, only one part of the warrior will be different, if any are: just one leg, or just the head, or just the torso.

If the head is deeper, the person has a strong sense of direction and self-confidence, and can make good decisions.

If the head is lighter, the person has trouble making decisions, or has lost his or her confidence and sense of direction. This is a sign of confusion.

If the torso is deeper, the person has a strong sense of purpose in life, strong convictions, and is able to weather any challenges or setbacks.

Head deeper

If the torso is lighter, the person lacks self-confidence and a sense of purpose, and needs encouragement.

The Arms

Head lighter

With the arms and legs, we return to the use of the four directions to interpret the figure. In Chapter 4, when we first met the warrior figure, we learned that one of its key features is that its limbs are oriented to the four directions. The right arm and leg of the figure align with the west, and the left arm and leg of the figure align with the east.

Torso deeper

If one arm or leg is drawn more deeply than the other, then the direction it represents is emphasized.

If the right arm is deeper, the person can best achieve personal ambition in a western direction. This could mean really west, as in California, or just west in the local sense. For instance, a warrior with the right arm deeper on an index finger knuckle might signify that the person's office is located west of his or her home, or that the territory of

Torso lighter

Right arm deeper

Left arm deeper

the job is located west of the home. This feature tells us that west is the direction to look to for success.

If the left arm is deeper, personal aims are best achieved in an eastern direction or setting.

Right leg deeper

If the right leg is deeper, a foundation for success will be found in a western direction or setting.

If the left leg is deeper, secure opportunity and a foundation for success lie in an eastern direction or setting.

Left leg deeper

The arms or legs of a warrior figure may not be even in length. Perhaps a right arm is longer than the left, or vice versa; the same with the legs. The long limb is a sign of opportunity and must be read for its direction.

Check the four limbs of a warrior figure to see if one arm or leg is longer than the other.

Right arm longer

If the right arm is longer, opportunity lies to the west. This feature is particularly useful when it's necessary to advise someone on a choice. For example, if a person has two job offers, one in San Francisco and the other in Chicago, and a warrior is found on an index finger knuckle with a longer right arm, this should be interpreted to mean the job in San Francisco will work out better, and is the preferred choice. It is as if the arm is pointing out the direction for success. Its length emphasizes that direction.

If the left arm is longer, opportunity lies to the east. We will learn in a later chapter how to make the most of a directional indicator by the questions we ask, to explore its possible significance.

Left arm longer

As an example, a person could be following his stocks and bonds, watching their progress. On the middle (financial) finger, a strong left arm on a warrior points to financial opportunity in the east. And east is where Wall Street lies, in New York. The warrior is a signal of success for the investments and points to further opportunity, a time for new investments. Those investments would suit the person's aims, as the arms represent a person's aims.

Right leg longer

Legs

If the right leg is longer, opportunity for a solid foundation for success lies in a western direction.

Left leg longer

If the left leg is longer, opportunity for solid success is found in an eastern direction.

Either leg substantially longer than the other is a signal for success in a southern direction. This is especially true if the leg is longer and more deeply drawn.

Either leg longer

Head

A most interesting feature is the occasional difference in the shape of the head of a warrior.

Circular head

Not all heads are circular in shape. Some are square or triangular.

A circular shape is normal and does not have a special meaning. A square head on a warrior is a sign of technical skills. A triangular head is a sign of a clever and inventive nature.

Square head

Look for any warrior with a triangle or square replacing the standard circle for the head, and know that this feature describes the person the warrior represents.

A warrior with a square head means that this person has above average technical skills. The person may be involved in science, and will especially like to work with computers.

Triangular head

A warrior with a triangular head means that this person is extraordinarily clever and shrewd, and does not "miss a trick" or "let any grass grow under his feet." This is a plus when it is found on a figure which represents anyone you must do business with, especially a partner or an investor.

OTHER CLUES

Analyzing the depth, length, and shape of a warrior's features is the first step to deciphering its message. Once we have an idea of a warrior's message, it is time to identify the person the warrior represents. Here are clues to a warrior's identity.

Dress

Most intriguingly, a warrior can be a unisex figure, drawn as described above, or a warrior can be clearly drawn as a male or female. The key to this feature is that some warriors wear clothes! The pattern is consistent: the males wear hats and the females wear skirts.

Imagine how useful this feature will be when you are trying to identify who the warrior represents. The dress provides an additional clue. Seemingly, when it is important to have further identification, the knuckles' figures obligingly put on a hat or a skirt to provide these extra clues.

The first step to identifying a figure is to keep in mind the finger on which the warrior is found. A warrior appearing on an index finger will be related to work. As an example, if a boss is represented on an index knuckle, the warrior figure could be a plain one or wear a hat, if the boss is male; and the warrior figure could be plain or wear a skirt, if the boss is female. Either type of figure will play the same role — represent the boss.

Placement

Every warrior in a knuckle can be identified by its placement. A minute ago, we saw that the limbs of a warrior figure are associated with the four directions. Geographical directions signaled by the limb's appearance are clues to the location of opportunity. However, the limbs and their directions are not used to identify the person the warrior represents, only the nature of the opportunity that the figure announces.

When we want to understand who the warrior represents, we will once again look to the four directions by studying where the warrior is placed in the knuckle. Every warrior figure will be located in one portion of the knuckle or another. And each portion of the knuckle has a direction assigned to it.

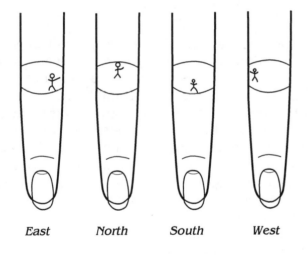

East   North   South   West

The placement in the knuckle of an entire figure, without any reference to the appearance of its limbs, will be a separate clue that helps to identify the figure.

The first step is to identify the finger on which the figure is found, to know if the warrior figure relates to someone at work (index finger), to someone concerned with our finances (middle finger), to someone in our personal lives (ring finger), or to someone with whom we negotiate (little finger).

The next step is to establish the location of the figure, and use that location as a starting point for identification. For instance, an uncle in Chicago would ideally be located in the northern part of the ring finger knuckle. An aunt in Savannah would be located in the southeastern part of the ring finger knuckle.

To analyze the warrior figures and then identify who they are, assign a meaning to their posture, assign a meaning to the depth of their features, the length of their limbs, and the shape of the heads.

Identification

Fingers' meaning: The meaning of the finger on which the figure is found identifies who it might be: someone connected with work, your money, your personal and emotional life, or your negotiating ability.

Geographical location: The geographical placement of the figure in the knuckle gives a further clue to the figure's identity.

Dress: The dress, although optional on a warrior, is another clue to the figure's identity, signifying a male or a female.

All of these rules apply to individual warrior figures. There is just one more point to the process of interpreting warriors.

Grouping: Most frequently warriors appear as single figures. But occasionally, warriors come in pairs, or even in groups of three or more. How to work with these figures? Exactly the same way as with the single figures, except for the fact that additional information comes from multiple figures: the interaction between the figures is also analyzed.

The most important feature to study is the posture of the group of warriors. What are they trying to tell you?

A pair of warriors could be standing in a friendly position, with hands and arms linked, or in an adversarial position, looking threatening or defensive. One figure might be taller than another.

The friendly pair is a symbol of cooperation. The figures might also stand for two actual people who relate well together. The adversarial pair is a symbol of friction, and may also represent two people in real life who are fighting. How will you know? By asking the client directly, to verify whether the client has two feuding people in his or her life right then. The pair who are different in height conveys the point that one figure is more powerful than the other. Height in a warrior is a symbol of dominance or authority.

All of the interpretations are straightforward and uncomplicated. The picture the figures present is read for what it is. The picture can be interpreted just as a mime's silent gestures would be interpreted.

Imagine a mime waving, or pointing to his or her heart, or leaping, or falling down. Any of these actions express a specific point the mime is making without words. The warriors act in just the same way, getting a point across silently but eloquently, according to the movement their posture portrays.

Once the warrior figures are analyzed and identified, the next step is to apply their message to the life of the person on whose hand the images are found.

17

Getting the Warriors' Message

Many of us have had the experience of going for a reading, and feeling that we want to hold back and be very careful not to reveal anything of ourselves. We want to see what our hands have to say, all on their own. Some of us want to test the person doing the interpretation. Others are just naturally reticent and private in nature.

In days past, when the atmosphere for readings was different, before the New Age, a reading was a real event. It was most often thought of as a psychic phenomenon, with the power to thrill and entertain. People wanted to believe that a veil could be lifted, and to the right practitioner, all their thoughts could be revealed.

Today, the atmosphere of a reading is more like that of a standard therapy session, with a client wanting to unburden certain thoughts and concerns, and the reader standing by, able to plug in, clarify, and possibly answer some of these concerns.

Today's consultations are a mixture of the two approaches, with the emphasis decidedly toward the therapy session. To put the art of reading in perspective, linking it with society's trends, just think of the widespread phenomenon of talk shows, with everyone eager to share their deepest, darkest secrets. People want to talk.

That trend is very convenient for our purposes. Because, to get the full benefit of the warriors' messages, all that information carried around in code form on your own hands has to be accessed through the creative process of give and take to sort out the signals the warriors give. Even to know who the warriors represent, a reader has to ask the client about the existence of people the warriors might symbolize.

Avoid withholding information to see if you, as a client, can make the reader tell you everything. Of course, this does not mean that you are obligated to tell everything you know, or even a fraction of it, when the person looking at your knuckles has questions. You have only to answer the question, giving a minimal response.

If you were asked, "Do you have a brother?" you can simply say "Yes." Not, "Yes, he lives in Cincinnati and his girlfriend is driving him crazy, she's pregnant and doesn't want an abortion and he doesn't want to get married because he thinks he might lose his job, because the company might shut down."

When a person working with your knuckles asks such a question, you can assume the reader thinks the figure that is the object of the question is your brother, or the reader would not have put the question that way. And you can answer the question with "yes" or "no." If the answer is "no," you and the reader do not waste time fixing attention on a nonexistent brother. The purpose of any question in the dialogue with a client is to clarify that the image in the knuckles corresponds to reality — or does not.

Each finger, you recall, relates to a specific area of your life. The image of a brother would properly be found on the ring finger, the finger relating to family, friends, and loved ones. This would be the reader's first clue. The next step is to ask you if a brother exists, to correspond to a warrior in the ring finger knuckle. If you have a figure in the knuckle and no brother in real life, there is the possibility the figure will relate to a close male friend, who acts as a brother in your life.

The point is, the reader must ask questions to establish the identity of any figure on any knuckle.

If you have ever given a deposition in a legal proceeding, you no doubt were instructed by your lawyer to give the shortest, least informative answer possible. Were you to volunteer too much information, you might get in a mess! You can treat your session with a person interpreting your knuckles in the same way.

Getting an interpretation of your knuckles is similar to another aspect of the lawyer's art — that of leading questions. In this process, a reader is going to ask you leading questions for every knuckle on every finger at the beginning, to help clarify the image on the knuckle.

When a lawyer asks a leading question, he or she has an agenda, a point in mind they are trying to establish by asking the question. A knuckle interpreter does the same. The reader sees with physical eyes what exists in the knuckle. The images are a fact, and are not an act of the reader's imagination — no matter how much we might wish for the reader to be performing as an incredible "psychic" — and the images are evidence of a story to be told. To sort out the evidence, to put the details into context, a reader must ask questions.

At this point, you might be asking, "But what about my fun? This sounds like a lot of work. I don't want to go to court, I just want to get my knuckles read."

It is true that the person receiving an interpretation of the knuckles does "work," and must be actively engaged in the process, not removed and distant, watching a spectacle unfold.

But the secret to this process is that until you have worked in this way, you have no idea how much fun it is to discover your reality encoded in your knuckles, with the help of the "seeing eyes" of the interpreter.

The images are so entertaining and informative that you find yourself lost in the information, unwilling to stop even for a second, and time flies by. The process, at its best, is so enveloping and intense that a tape recording of the session should be made, to give you a chance to hear the information again later and absorb it at leisure.

The entertainment comes from the amazement and near disbelief you will feel that so much of your world is sitting literally at your fingertips, waiting to be revealed and acknowledged.

You know more than you think you know; more than you could ever be consciously aware of. You have a great deal stored away in your mind. Recall how we looked in Chapter 8 at the brain's ability, on an unconscious level, to scan our environment and collect pieces of information that we could never know by ordinary channels, using the five ordinary senses. The brain's ability to gather and store information goes beyond the action of our five senses.

Reading the knuckles is one way to add to our conscious knowledge from the storehouse of our unconscious knowledge. This translation from the world of the unconscious through its symbols, into the world of the conscious mind through the reader's words, is what makes the images compelling as they and their significance unfold through the reading process.

Perhaps working with the warriors and symbols in the knuckles is one of the quickest ways to access our unconscious knowledge. Other therapeutic arts accomplish the same thing, only more slowly.

The point of therapy is to gain conscious awareness of and control over certain behavior patterns. The point of working with the knuckles is to gain conscious knowledge of certain facts that may be useful to us.

All of this must be more fascinating than sitting for a "circus" with the old expectations of being entertained during a reading. Knuckle work is a more sophisticated approach to answering life's questions, because of the nature of the dialogue it entails.

So, how do we do it? We are going to start our hunt for warriors on the index finger, proceed to the middle finger, then move to the ring finger, and finally, reach the little finger. We are going to do this for each hand. As we work with each knuckle, we are always going to be aware of what finger we are examining, and we will use the meaning of that finger to give us a clue to the identity of the figure.

Three simple steps start the journey to using the warriors as guides to reality. First, look at the knuckle. Next, decide what you see; and then ask questions. We will discuss these steps in detail.

Look at the knuckle: Spend a few minutes looking thoroughly at the knuckle you have chosen to view. Keep in mind what finger the knuckle is found on, and know that the area of life the finger represents will determine in what category the figure belongs.

A. Warriors on the index knuckle: Assume they are work-related. Is the figure a boss, a co-worker, or an employee?

B. Warriors on the middle finger knuckle: Assume they are finance-related. Is the figure a banker, broker, insurance agent, a lender, a borrower, an investment partner, or involved in any other way with finances?

C. Warriors on the ring finger knuckle: Assume they are part of your personal life. Is the figure a friend, lover, spouse, child, relative, enemy, acquaintance?

D. Warriors on the little finger knuckle: Assume they are someone you have dealt with on a formal or an informal basis, to get something done. It could be anyone from a maintenance man to your Wall Street broker. The negotiating finger figures have the widest possible interpretation, because we deal with a number of people for a variety of reasons.

Decide what you see: Determine what you find in a knuckle. One warrior? Two? A pair of them together? Any warrior with a hat or a skirt, revealing gender? A tall and a short warrior? You may not find a warrior in every knuckle. Do not expect that. We work with all the knuckles, using shape and color, and intepret the warriors when we find them.

Ask questions: In your own mind, begin to decide what you want to make of the figures you have found. What questions do you have about the figures? What do you want to know in order to be able to communicate to the client the message of each warrior and its posture? Your first step in the dialogue is to ask an opening question that will help identify each figure.

Here is a list of good opening questions, to help establish the identity of a figure you are seeing on a particular finger.

Index finger	Do you have a boss, coworker, or colleague you work closely with?
Middle finger	Do you have a business partner? A banker? A landlord? A broker? Another financial figure in your life?
Ring finger	Do you have a wife/husband, boyfriend/girlfriend? (And if the figure is small) a child? (If the figure looks tall) parents or grandparents?
Little finger	Do you have anyone you are working on a project or a deal with? A client? A business partner? A neighbor or club member?

Use the meaning of the finger on which the figure is found as a guideline for your question. If you are working with the index finger and find a tall warrior, signifying authority, ask the person about his boss, as a starting point. Make sure he has a boss, and that the tall figure does not instead represent a partner or a coworker. You will only know that if you ask, because we are assuming you have not met this client before, and you are not doing a psychic reading. You are only preparing to convey the story of the warrior according to his posture and location in the knuckle.

Alternate Line of Questioning

If your first questions centered on the meaning of the fingers do not identify the warrior figures, you can extend the line of your questioning. As it happens, a boyfriend or wife could work in the same office as your client. In this case, the person might show up on the index finger as well as on the relationship finger, the ring finger. A grandparent who leaves money to your client will often show up on the middle finger as well as on the ring finger. A child who is in the same line of work as a parent can show up on the parent's index finger. A child who is supported financially by a parent can show up on the middle finger, as well as on the ring finger.

To look a bit deeper to find out who a figure on a knuckle represents, you can factor in family members as your second attempt at identification.

The following questions are a good way to continue dialogue for the fingers.

Index finger	Do you have a family member who works?
Middle finger	Do you have a family member involved with your money?
Little finger	Do you have a project you are working on with a family member?

Notice we have left out the ring finger in the list — because that is where family belongs! You expect to find them there. On the contrary, you do not expect to find work or business figures on the ring finger. The subject matter of that finger is more personal.

The basic treatment of a figure, however, is to assume it is related to the area of life that the finger represents. Once you have that orientation established and the figure identified through your questions, then you can look for other details.

1. Where in the knuckle is the figure located?

2. What is its posture?

3. What do the details of the figure tell you?

The Figures' Location

The location will help you further identify the figures. As a good starting point, when you look at any knuckle, check the area that represents your city or state first — the area where you and the person having the knuckles read live. That area should

have a figure in it on at least one of the knuckles.

Let's try a few samples of finding and interpreting a figure located in the area where you and the client live. Let's say you are working with the index finger and the figure represents a boss.

You and your client live in Texas. The figure on the index knuckle is found as seen in the illustration to the left.

The boss is in a victory posture. This means he or she has achieved a lot in his or her work.

Next, let's say you and your client live in Florida. The figure on the index knuckle will be found as shown on the right.

The figure looks strong. That tells you that all is well with your clients' boss' career.

Now, let's say you and your client live in Seattle. The figure on the index knuckle is found as shown below to the right.

The boss' aggressive posture tells you he or she works hard to beat the competition, or to climb the ladder of success.

Once you have dealt with the boss, be aware of other outstanding figures, those that catch your eye in any area of the knuckle.

If there are figures in both the area where you are located and in another area, deal with the one closest to home first, as we just did with the boss. Then try to identify the second figure.

Let's assume you find two figures in the index finger knuckle: a tall warrior in the north sector, where you live, and another figure in the east sector.

The tall warrior in the north sector will most likely be the boss, and you will establish that with your questions to your client. Then you will need to figure out who the figure in the east represents. It could be your boss' boss, if the company headquarters are located in the east.

Both figures are work related. You begin to find out who the figure in the east is by asking your client, "Are your headquarters in the east?" If so, the figure will also represent the headquarters, and the person who heads it. A warrior does multiple duties, in many cases.

You continue, "Does the company do a lot of business in the east?" If so, that figure could represent a major client for the company. Or, "Do you ever work with someone in the east?" If so, that figure could represent the person your client works with in the east.

The Figures' Posture

Now for the fun part. What is the first figure's posture? A victory posture? Then since that describes the boss, you know your client's boss has a victory, or at least smooth sailing, ahead. What about the other figure in the east? Does it also have a victory posture? Say the figure represents both your boss and the company headquarters. You know the company will do well when the second figure is also in a victory posture.

Try it another way. Your client's boss has a defeated posture. This means the boss has a problem or a challenge ahead. The second figure is in a victory posture. This means he or she could be of help to your boss, or that the company's general progress will support your boss. If both figures have a defeated posture, then you know this represents a difficult period for both the boss and the company.

One more variation. Your client's boss is in a victorious posture, and the second figure is in a defeated posture. This means that while your client's boss' performance is strong, the company may develop difficulties — or your boss' boss will have a challenge.

Don't be put off by all these variations. In person, the dialogue is not hard to come up with because the figures you see inspire the questions. Just take your clue from what you see in the knuckle.

The Figures' Details

Remember that you can check the heads for shape and depth, the torso for depth, and the limbs for length and depth. Let's say your client's boss has a triangular head. This means the boss is very clever and will get ahead. Let's say the auxiliary figure has a square head. That means your client's boss' boss is practical and excellent in technical skills. Now consider this. If the two peoples' heads are shaped differently, this could mean a basic incompatibility between the two. But as long as the two figures are in a positive posture, the incompatibility will not be an issue.

As another example of how the details of the warriors' posture tell a story, let's say your client's boss has a deeply drawn head. This means the boss is confident and happy with his or her career direction. Let's say the torso of the second figure is strong. That means the company is in good shape. If the second figure's torso is weak, then the company may develop problems. If your client's boss' arms are deeply drawn, the boss can achieve his or her aims. If the second figure's legs are long and deeply drawn, then the company has a solid foundation.

So, with just two figures on an index knuckle, you have been able to see the prospects of a boss and his or her boss, as well as those of the company itself. Quite a lot of information from just two warrior figures.

For any figure, on any finger, you will always use the triple-header source of information: location in the knuckle, posture of the warrior, and details about the individual limbs on the warrior.

You can say so much with just a tiny scrap of physical evidence. Let's recap what you might have been asking during this exchange.

EXAMPLE DIALOGUES FOR THE INDEX FINGER

When you first found the tall figure in the index knuckle, you would ask, "Do you have a boss?" We assumed in the above exchange that it was the boss, for the purposes of an example. But let's be open to all possibilities with our dialogue. The person may say, "No, I own my own company." In this case, you next ask, "Do you have a strong or competent person working for you?" That is the leading question you come up with, since the figure is tall. If the figure you found were drawn with weak arms and a light head, you would ask, "Do you have someone working for you who can never get anything done, and who lacks a clear sense of direction?"

Or the person might respond, "No, I have a partner." Then the figure obviously stands for the partner. Read its posture to find out how the partner is faring. Always take your cue from the person who answers your questions. You must be able to constantly adapt the information you see objectively engraved in those knuckles.

Going back to our example assumption that the first figure in the north represents your client's boss, you might ask, "Does your boss work in the east?" If yes, then ask, "Are the company headquarters in the east?" If yes, then ask, "Does your boss have a boss in the east?" If yes, then your information is complete and you can begin to read the figures' posture and details.

Those are sample questions you will ask. Next, you will tell the client what you are seeing in the knuckles. As an example, "Your boss is drawn here in a posture that indicates victory. He or she is very tall, and looks confident in this drawing." You can continue, "Because the arms are deeply drawn, the boss will achieve his or her aims." And, "Because his boss' legs are also long and deeply drawn, the company is on a good footing, has a solid foundation, and you can expect a successful association with both your boss and the company."

Here are dialogue possibilities which really make you stretch to learn all the ways to identify a figure. Take it slowly. This is not as complicated as it may seem, but only logical guesses about the figures.

EXAMPLE DIALOGUES FOR THE MIDDLE FINGER

Let's say you have two warrior figures of equal height, side by side, with hands linked.

The posture indicates a cooperative spirit between the two figures, and the fact that the figures are the same height indicates that one is not dominant over the other.

Your first question to your client might be, "Do you have a partner in a business venture?" If so, then the symbol speaks well of the way the two work together, and predicts success for the investments. You might also ask, "Are you satisfied with the way your finances are going?" If yes, then that pair symbolizes the good flow and even circumstances for the person's finances.

As you can see, the symbols can stand for more than one aspect of reality, and for more than one person. Your job is to identify the most likely person involved, represented by the warrior, then to think of meanings other than those based on people. The cooperative figures in this instance should ideally stand for a real life person who works well with your client, and for conditions in the business world.

Example Dialogues for the Ring Finger

Let's try another example. This sample is meant to address several possible ways to identify the figures. Say you are working with a client, and you find two figures in a ring finger knuckle. One is a female warrior, wearing a skirt, and the other a tiny warrior figure, obviously a child, in a dependent posture alongside the bigger figure.

You have not met this woman client before. Your first thought on seeing a female warrior and child image is that perhaps they are a mother-child combination since the little figure looks dependent on the larger figure.

But first you need to know who the large figure is. The female warrior will not represent the woman client herself, because warriors represent others in our lives. The next most logical guess would be for the warrior to be someone, almost an alter ego, for the client, a sister or a friend who is as close as a sister. You ask the woman, "Do you have a sister?" No, is the answer. Go on to your next best guess. "Do you have a close friend who has a child?" If yes, then you have identified the figure.

Let's back up. You ask, "Do you have a sister?" The answer might be "Yes." but you may get this: "Well, I have two sisters and they both have a child." You then ask, knowing that you see a dependent posture on the little figure, "Well, does one of your sisters have a child who is either very young or very dependent on her?" You will most likely get an affirmative answer to this. If by any chance, the client responds that both sisters' children are young and dependent, then you must try to isolate which sister the figure represents. You can ask, "Are you closer to one sister than the other?" If yes, then this helps identify the figure. If no, then look to the location of the figures. Say they are located in the same area where you and the person you are speaking with live. You ask, "Do both your sisters live in the area?" If you're lucky, one does and one does not. The one who lives close by geographically is then the designated sister. You will want to be sure you are referring to the right mother-child combination before you begin to give out the story the warrior tells. Undoubtedly, your client is going to use the information, and might just inform the sister of what you said. You want the right sister to get the message!

The image is an opening for a dialogue about the mother and child, whoever they may be. Perhaps your client will say, "Oh, I was just thinking about them. Suzy's child has to start kindergarten, and is afraid to leave home." You can verify that from the child figure's posture, but reassure your client all will go well, if the mother figure looks strong, as if she can reassure the child in turn. Also the child figure could have a strong head, or arms deeply drawn, even if the posture were clingy. This is a sign that the child will do all right in her new circumstances.

Or perhaps your client will say, "I'm not aware that my sister's child feels dependent or is clingy. He seems quite strong, really." This is your opportunity to inform her that the child does have some hesitancy or reservation about facing life, all appearances to the contrary.

Later when the child is questioned or carefully monitored, most likely a true slant on the child's feelings will come up, and your client will say, "Oh yes, she told me little Johnny was afraid to go to school." If fact, you may not have said exactly that, but only that Johnny was feeling afraid or cautious about something, as that's what his posture conveyed.

Your client was unconsciously picking up on the child's feelings, and the reality was printed out in her knuckle. Let's assume her sister did not know her child felt fearful about something. By bringing this to conscious awareness, you were able to help facilitate a clearing up of the child's circumstances. That is the purpose of the reading, to help and clarify wherever possible and wherever needed.

And in the meantime, your client gets to have the extraordinary experience of finding out a useful piece of information from her knuckles, and you have the satisfaction of delivering it.

Notice that in our two examples, we first made the child a girl and then a boy. Because no gender specifications were on the child figure, no hat or skirt, we do not know the gender. All we know from the drawing is that there is one child involved. Because the issue was the child's dependent nature, the image printed on the knuckle contains this information. The images are selective. The gender of the child would not be important, only his or her state of mind. The knuckles always print out only the essential information in any image.

The more you work with the knuckle's images, the more you will appreciate the economy, efficiency, and directness of the images. These qualities greatly help you to get your job done.

Example Dialogues for the Little Finger

In this case, let's say you have a male client sitting in front of you. On his little finger knuckle, you find a warrior located in the area where you both live, and the warrior has a victory posture.

You ask the client if he is in sales. If yes, then you ask him if he has recently made a successful sale. If so, then that figure represents the person who bought your client's product or services. You might also find out from the client that he has just

secured a new account as well as the large sale first mentioned. The symbols can also be taken to mean that your client's ability to negotiate — in other words, to sell — is on the upswing.

If there were a warrior in the appropriate area with a secretive or skulking posture (as illustrated on the next page), you would ask the client if he is dealing with someone he does not feel comfortable with.

If the client answers yes, you can confirm that the client's

uncomfortable feelings are on tar-
get, as the warrior figure looks
secretive, or not quite above board.

If the client says that he is comfortable with everyone he deals with,
then you have to warn him to be on
the lookout for an unexpected turn
in his dealings with someone. You
will not be able to tell him who to
watch out for, as the figure cannot
be identified if the client has no conscious awareness of problems with
anyone in his business. But what you
can do is give him a time frame for
how long he must be on guard against any unfa-
vorable developments with a person he deals with.

In a minute we will look at time frames for the
warriors. But first, let's go back and give the figures
from our four sample dialogues the simplest possible interpretation. To the client you say:

"You have two strong figures around you in
your work. From their posture, I predict success for
you and the company."

"You have two harmonious figures in your
money finger knuckle. This means your finances
are in good shape."

"You have a mother and child figure in your
ring finger knuckle, and the child appears to need
protection, which the mother is capable of giving."

"You have a figure in a victory posture in your little finger knuckle. This means your negotiations produce favorable results."

We still haven't named a time frame for the above actions. The time frame assigned to the knuckle on which the image appears will be used to add that detail to the picture, if you wish to be more precise. You can work without the timing if you want to spark discussion using images alone. Timing, however, is essential if you want to make predictions.

The Appropriate Time Frame

With what we know now, we can begin to use the time frame each knuckle offers. So far, we have reviewed only the basic rules for interpreting and identifying the warrior figures. We have not gone beyond that to use the other features of our system.

Remember your time frames. The past of a year or more ago is on the middle or background knuckles on the nondominant hand; the recent past of six months ago is on the tip or catalyst knuckles of the nondominant hand. The future for the nondominant hand is up to two or three years ahead. On the dominant hand, we have the present in the middle knuckles, and the future, six to eighteen months ahead, on the tip knuckles.

Let's put the example from the index finger dialogue, page 240, on the present knuckle. That means all the discussion about the boss, the boss' boss, and the company's prospects are true for now, from today up to two or three months ahead.

We'll put the previous example from the middle finger on the middle set of knuckles, on the nondominant hand. The cooperative symbol for the client's finances is good for a time frame of one year ago and up to three years ahead, maximum. That means the positive nature of the client's finances is well-established.

Put the last example from the ring finger knuckle on the tip knuckles of the nondominant hand. The dependent child and reassuring mother figures are in a situation that has been developing over the last six months and will smooth out in the next three years ahead, maximum.

To put the final example from the little finger dialogue on the tip knuckles, the future knuckles, on the dominant hand, we have to alter the dialogue a little bit, asking, "Do you have a good sale or a new account pending, that you expect to materialize in the next six months or so?" And if the client says yes, you can reply that his expectations will be met, and that it will all work out as planned. If the client says, no, he's not anticipating a sale or a new account in six months, then you have the happy task of informing him that he's got great news ahead, for he will get the sale and the new account.

You work with the warriors by analyzing their posture and the details of their features, and by their location in the knuckle, which helps to identify them. We talk with the client to confirm the actual existence of the figures drawn in the knuckles.

From the results of the dialogue plus the location of the warrior, you put the pieces of the puzzle together. You are able to describe people and conditions in the client's life and predict an outcome for them — all because the brain cares enough to print these images in the knuckles, and you know enough to begin to decode them.

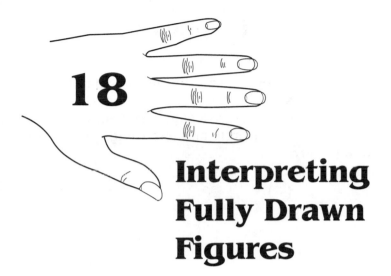

18

Interpreting Fully Drawn Figures

Images in the knuckles are a window on our unconscious knowledge of the world around us. Three types of figures, or images, let us "view the action": warriors, fully drawn figures, and symbols.

These three designs, each with their own messages, provide guidelines to the knuckles' meaning. Let's look at the pattern of each type of figure, and its role and interpretation, before we concentrate exclusively on fully drawn figures and symbols in the pages to follow.

WARRIORS

Warriors get their name from the fact that they look like warriors.

Warriors, in their design, are simplicity itself. They need only a circle and a few lines put together in a pattern.

ROLE OF THE WARRIOR

The warrior is an action figure. Its dynamic posture in the knuckle tells a tale that reveals the action in our world. The warrior's image on a knuckle most directly reveals the essence of the world, because the warrior's role is to be in the world. A warrior contends with the world and its forces. Its message, sent through the image on a knuckle, is meant to help a person contend with his or her world. The warrior's posture and the meaning of the finger on which it is found are the main guidelines to interpretation. Location of the warrior and details of its figure add to the interpretation.

INTERPRETING THE WARRIOR

Who does the warrior represent? What does it represent? A warrior is a human figure, and depicts male and female, adult and child, as well as unisex figures, who represent people in real life. For purposes of interpretation, a warrior first represents real people; then, as a secondary meaning, a warrior represents situations or events, as we saw in the previous chapter.

There, one of our warriors stood for a boss' boss, the company headquarters, and even the general progress of the company. The string of associations starts first with a real life person, then extends to include anything connected with that person.

FULLY DRAWN FIGURES

Fully drawn figures need more than sticks for limbs, as they are modeled on a more lifelike picture of the people they represent. They are not abstract designs. The best way to describe these fully drawn figures is to call them cartoon figures, as that is what they look like: little, round, puffy figures, with an animated look to them.

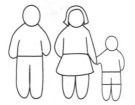

They are capable of illustrating whole scenes, and are often found in multiples — two or three grouped together.

ROLE OF THE FULLY DRAWN (CARTOON) FIGURE

Fully drawn figures resemble a painting or photograph, a still life piece of reality that reminds one of the saying, "a picture is worth a thousand words." These figures are not active, as warriors are. Their role is to describe people more fully, primarily through extra details of dress. These figures are dressed up, either in today's styles or in the garb of any era in history. Dress ranges anywhere from that of a few decades ago, back to ancient Greek and Roman times. If dress is contemporary, the figure represents a real life person. A costume from another era represents psychological traits. If a person were drawn in a Renaissance outfit, for example, that drawing would indicate that the person is idealistic and romantic by nature.

The role of cartoon figures is two-fold: to further identify the people in the knuckles, and to expand upon details of a person's character and psychology. Interpreting knuckles is meant to give a better understanding of our world and the people in it who affect our lives. This is what cartoon figures do — help us understand people in our lives more thoroughly.

These figures are richer in detail than the warriors are. While warriors are drawn only as human figures, cartoon figures include humans and animals. The reason for this difference lies in the purpose of each design. Warriors are meant to convey action, and cartoon figures are used to describe relationships.

To illustrate the purpose of an animal drawn as a cartoon figure, think for a moment of a Christmas card with a family photo. The photo conveys greetings through its image of the family sending the card. The family poses in a way that best represents their unit. And how often the family unit includes a pet — a dog, a cat, a pony! Such a photo says it all about the role of animals in human lives. This close association of humans and animals, their relationship, also comes across in knuckles' images.

INTERPRETING THE CARTOON FIGURES

Who do the cartoon figures represent? Human cartoon figures represent real people in real life. These figures include male and female, adult and child, and refer only to people. A cartoon person never refers to an animal.

Animal cartoon figures are more diverse. An animal can represent an actual animal, or be a stand-in for a human figure. A cat, for instance, may represent a real cat, the family pet. Or a cat can represent a person, and the message is that the qualities of a cat — curiosity, for example — describe the person.

We are going to look at the rules for interpreting cartoon figures shortly.

SYMBOLS

Symbols are the only type of knuckle images that do not feature human figures. Symbols are free-form graphics depicting geometric shapes, scenery, and everyday items. Examples of these are a triangle, an ocean, and a flag or tent.

ROLE OF THE SYMBOLS

The symbols are a further way of identifying people in the knuckles, although they do so indirectly. The direct meaning of symbols in knuckles is connected to places. The role of symbols is to name places. Places include more geographical information, which is meant to indicate countries, states, and cities. Places identified by the knuckles' symbols also include settings, such as mountains and the beach. A place might be important in itself, or only because it is associated with a person.

The second and most outstanding role of a symbol is to announce opportunity through the use of two special creatures: fish and birds. The fish is the major symbol of opportunity for the person in whose knuckle it is found. The fish represents a "catch" just as vital and important as fish were to primitive people in the days before crops and farms. A bird is the knuckle's way of pointing out an opportunity "on the wing," something that could easily come the person's way and be of advantage. The bird shares in the primitive nature of the knuckles' opportunity signals, as birds were also essential to early people who relied directly on nature for sustenance.

Taken together, warriors, fully drawn figures, and symbols provide a world of information about our lives, and the people and conditions that shape them.

To work with the remaining two types of figures, we need to find and identify them. Along the way, we will also note the differences between these figures and the warriors.

WORKING WITH FULLY DRAWN FIGURES

You already know how to locate warriors in the knuckles and what to do with them. The first step is simply to look at the knuckles and see what you can find in each of them. This time, rather than looking for warriors, you are going to concentrate on finding fully drawn figures as you scan the entire surface of the knuckle.

FINDING FULLY DRAWN FIGURES

Look for a circle, which is a telltale clue, to help you find the head of a figure. Once you have spotted a circle, which could be the head of a fully drawn figure, follow the image downward to see if you find a continuation of the figure — a neck, shoulders, a body dressed in some style, and arms. Continue to look down to see if you can find legs, and perhaps feet.

These fully drawn figures may not include the entire length of the body. At times you will find figures drawn from the waist up, or only from the shoulders up. This is why it is a good idea to look for the head first, as it must be present to anchor the figure.

Finally, be alert for cartoon figures which are grouped in pairs, or come in freestanding groups of two, three, or four figures. Multiple cartoon figures are more common than multiple warrior figures. The reason for this is that these figures are meant to depict relationships, while a single warrior figure can do its job — portray action — alone.

DIFFERENCES IN THE APPEARANCE OF WARRIORS AND CARTOON FIGURES

There are some differences in the way warrior and cartoon figures are drawn.

The head: A cartoon figure must always have a head, which is the first clue to its existence in a knuckle. A warrior figure very often has a circle (or a square or triangle) for a head, but can be found without any of these forms. The straight line extension of the torso on a warrior can serve as a head.

Depth: A warrior figure almost always is drawn more deeply in the knuckle, while a cartoon figure is etched more faintly. This means that looking for the deepest lines first will most likely yield warriors, and fainter lines will form the image of cartoon figures.

Limbs: Because a warrior gets his message across through his posture, he needs his limbs. A warrior missing both legs would have a very incomplete message (and would most likely be unable to do his job, if he were a real figure!). But because the body of a cartoon figure is not meant to express action and movement, because the arms and legs could be covered by dress details, their limbs are not a point of focus, and often are not seen in full view.

DIFFERENCES IN THE INTERPRETATION OF WARRIORS AND CARTOON FIGURES

There are different ways to interpret warrior and cartoon figures. We analyze warriors by their posture, the depth of their features, the length of their limbs, and shape of their heads. We identify them through the meaning of the finger, their location on the knuckle, and their dress. The significance of their grouping is not a major point of interpretation, but incidental to other, essential points.

But, with cartoon figures, which often appear in multiples, the way the figures are grouped is a key point of interpretation. To analyze cartoon figures, we also concentrate on their dress and the way the images face in the knuckle. To identify who a cartoon figure represents in real life, we use location and the meaning of the finger, just as with the warriors, as well as the dress. Dress, or the way a cartoon figure is clothed, will be used both to identify and to analyze the figure.

ANALYZING FULLY DRAWN (CARTOON) FIGURES

To analyze fully drawn figures, we concentrate on profile, dress, and grouping.

Profile

The main difference in the analysis of these figures is that we do not analyze their posture, as we do for warriors, but concentrate instead on how the figure faces in the knuckle: does the figure face forward, with the front of the figure visible; or does

Front

Back

Side

the figure face backward, with the back visible; or does the figure face the side, which is a position commonly labeled "profile"?

The way the figure is placed in the knuckle is its profile in the sense that the figure's positioning, or its profile, is how the figure makes itself known. Each position has a specific interpretation.

Figure facing front: This position signals a welcoming attitude. Any figure facing forward in the knuckle's image is "here to stay." A forward facing figure represents a person who is committed, reliable, "in for the long haul," friendly, and interested in engaging with other people. For instance, if a boyfriend is represented by a figure facing forward, he would be a solid bet, committed, and intending to remain in the relationship.

Figure facing back: This position signals a dissatisfied or unhappy attitude. A figure which presents its back to view is "on the way out." This position is a "good-bye" signal, a sign of impermanence, and can be used to predict a relationship or situation that is going to end. The unconscious knowledge of this is printed out in a graphic signal on the knuckle. If a boyfriend figure presents his back to view, the boyfriend in question is not happy with the relationship and is not likely to stay in it much longer, or at least not permanently.

Figure facing to the side: This position signals a flexible attitude. The person represented by this figure wants to keep his or her options open. A figure facing sideways can be interpreted as "looking over the territory." If this figure were a boyfriend, his attitude would be open and flexible. He might be reviewing all his options in the relationship.

To sum it up, a forward-facing figure wants to stay with a situation, a backward-facing figure wants to leave, and a figure facing to the side wants to keep options open.

Dress

The way a figure is dressed sends out important signals. Dress on fully drawn figures serves a dual purpose. First and most obviously, dress shows gender. Pants and suits are found on male figures; skirts, dresses, and gowns on female figures. Second, dress is a way of portraying personality characteristics, and it is these characteristics with which we are concerned as we analyze the figures.

To work with dress, we use these guidelines:

1. The type of dress as a guide to age and personality of the figure

2. Contemporary dress versus period dress as a guide to character traits

3. Hats as a guide to activities, status, and personality

Type of dress (female figures): Dress can consist of apparel from the most informal to the most formal types: from bathing suits to short skirts, to average-length skirts, to long skirts. Dresses and gowns can also vary in length. The

length of the apparel is a signal for the age and attitude of the person represented. A short skirt on
any type of dress signals a youthful person or a
casual attitude. A long skirt, on the other hand, is a
signal for an older person or a reserved demeanor.
An average-length skirt on any piece of clothing
means a more conventional personality, and does
not specify an age. Any informal-looking outfit
means a younger or happy-go-lucky type of person.
A formal outfit, a gown, or a coat with hat and
gloves means an older person, someone of stature
and authority. If formal dress stands for stature
and authority, then the age of the person is not
emphasized. A 29-year-old woman who heads a
department could be represented in a formal
gown. So could a 65-year-old matron. Age or
authority is the signal of formal wear.

Type of dress (male figures): Dress consists
of pants, shirts, suits, coats, and hats, ranging from
the most informal to the most formal type: from
swimsuit trunks to short pants, to a pants and shirt
outfit, to a suit, to an overcoat, to a tuxedo and top
hat. The guidelines are the same as for female
dress — the more formal the outfit, the older or
more important the person. An informal outfit signals a casual attitude or a younger male.

Contemporary dress versus period dress:
Although certain features of dress are consistent
and lend themselves to a set interpretation, the
variety of dress is incredible. A distinct category is
contemporary versus period dress. Contemporary
dress is read directly for what it is, casual or formal, while costume dress is used to highlight special qualities in the personality. The qualities
associated with the costume belong to the person:

idealism in the case of a Renaissance outfit; an adventurous nature for a person pictured in a safari outfit. The possibilities are endless. Each costume has to be read for what it is.

The most frequently found costume imagery centers on a popular theme: knights and their ladies. Men appear in knights' armor, and ladies in long gowns, with tall, cone-shaped hats. The knight is often pictured riding a horse. This image, above all, represents a romantic and idealistic nature, a crusader at heart, a fighter for what is right.

Figures appear in religious garb with the clothes of a monk, or even of a bishop with a tall hat. Many women seem to wear a veil. They could represent nuns or Arabs! The tendency to keep themselves apart from men and the world is the characteristic that identifies these women.

Hats: Most often male figures wear hats. Occasionally female figures wear hats. The purpose of a hat on these figures is not to specify gender but to reveal many things: personality, activities, interests, pursuits, vocations; to indicate stature and accomplishment, and to describe situations that are in progress, not yet complete — under wraps, in other words.

A figure of either sex wearing a hat is revealed to be secretive in nature. The phrase "keep it under your hat" applies to them. A figure with a hat does not lay all his cards on the table. Any type of hat carries this meaning.

The variety of hats that figures wear is astonishing, and often whimsical as they tell their tale. A specific kind of hat always adds information about the personality of the figure, as well as giving a list of interests, pursuits, and vocations.

Examples are helmets on a soldier figure or a policeman, a conductor's cap, a pilot's cap, a fireman's hat, a chef's hat, a bishop's hat, fishing hat, baseball cap, safari hat; and a hat frequently found on figures, one in the Sherlock Holmes style, which indicates a person with a strong sense of curiosity, and ability as an investigator.

In some cases, a hat is a symbol of glory on a figure, of having reached a pinnacle in life, usually in a career. Any hat, apart from casual and sport styles, is a symbol of authority. The more formal the hat, such as a top hat, the more complete the authority and higher the status. Often, a tall hat or a top hat is used to designate the boss. Appearing on any figure, a tall hat reveals competence.

Finally, in keeping with the idea that something under a hat is "under wraps," or not fully revealed, a figure in a hat can represent a situation that is developing, or in progress. For example, two figures on a ring finger knuckle just starting a relationship could wear hats to indicate that more is yet to come in the relationship.

In summary, these four points are covered by hats:

1. Personality traits

2. Activities, pursuits, interests, vocations

3. Figures of authority and competence

4. Situations not yet complete

Grouping

Fully drawn figures resemble cartoon characters not only for the puffy, round look of the clothed images, but also for their tendency to appear in multiple numbers, creating a scene which tells a story. Cartoon figures in a newspaper rarely appear alone: Beetle Bailey has his sergeant; Garfield has his owner; Snoopy has Charlie, Lucy, and a host of other friends. What makes a story in a cartoon strip, and in the knuckles, poignant is the ins and outs of the relationship between the characters.

The tendency of the knuckles' cartoon figures to appear in numbers reflects their role as indicators of relationships between people. This is the point of the groupings in the knuckles: to give further details about a relationship in any given area of life, professional, social, or personal.

There are two basic attitudes the figures reflect: either a bonding and joining together, indicating harmony; or a pulling apart, or facing different angles, indicating disharmony. Here are a few examples of how to interpret figures by their profiles and how closely together they stand.

Two figures facing forward is a symbol of a solid relationship, and the ability to agree on any matter.

One figure facing forward, another facing backward indicates two people who have different points of view and may not be able to come to terms.

Two figures standing side by side, touching, is another symbol of close union and harmony.

Facing forward

One forward, one back

Side by side

Pulling away

Difference in height

Two figures pulling away from each other is an indication that the relationship is strained and may come apart.

As we did with the warriors, we can use the height of the figures, if different, to gauge who is the senior member or the physically older person in the pair. The taller person is either of an older generation, or more important than the shorter figure.

Cartoon figures also come in threes and fours, and the basic rules for two figures also apply to them. Are all the figures facing the same direction? If so, there is harmony in the group. If two figures are facing forward and a third is facing backward, one member of the group is not in harmony with the other two. If they represented three partners in a business, the one facing backward could be expected to withdraw from the partnership. If the other two partners were unaware of the third person's dissatisfaction, a warning from the knuckles' figures could save the day. The two could take action to avoid a split, or if unavoidable, make the transition a smooth one, with advance warning.

Rules for height apply to any multiple figures. The tallest one in the group will represent the senior person, or the most important one.

All that remains is to look at the ways to identify fully drawn figures.

Three points will cover this detail:

1. Use the meaning of the finger on which the figure is found

2. Locate the figure geographically

3. Notice the dress

Identifying fully drawn cartoon figures is done in the same way as the warriors, using the meaning of the finger to determine the area of life and the geographical area the figure belongs to, as a possible means of identifying it. Dress on these figures is more revealing than that on the warriors, however.

The differences in dress that help us analyze the figures and their attitude can be used to identify a person literally. A mother figure is likely to be someone's mother; an older person, a grandparent; a younger person, a child, niece, or nephew; and so on. The rule for literal interpretation is if the figure looks like a parent, a grandparent, or a child, it probably is one. The way to know for sure is to ask the client once the dialogue has started, as we saw with the warriors.

Sample dialogues for the full figures will be found in the last chapter.

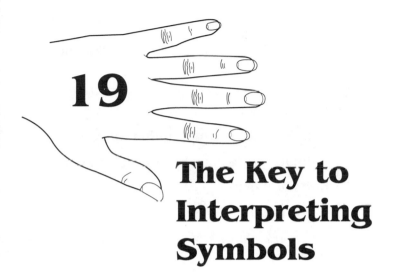

19

The Key to Interpreting Symbols

Symbols in the knuckles are a fascinating study. Little pictures, formed by distinct lines that organize themselves into recognizable shapes, reveal as much about our world as the warriors and cartoon figures do. The difference between the figures we have already seen and the symbols lies in the direct way information is given out. We can read the figures directly, using their posture and dress as a source of meaning. To interpret the symbols we have to stretch a bit, because symbols are more abstract than figures, and their interpretation is not always as obvious.

To understand symbols as they appear in the knuckles, here is a summary of the main types and how to interpret them.

Symbols consist of:

1. Geometric shapes: squares, rectangles, triangles, circles

2. Drawings of everyday items: tents, huts, bowls, boats, etc.

3. Scenery: clouds, mountains, oceans

4. Animals: any domestic or wild animal

5. Birds and fish

THE SYMBOLS' USE

How do we use the symbols? The symbols' main function is to reveal places, like countries, states, and areas of the world; physical surroundings like mountains and oceans; and, through birds and fish, to indicate opportunity.

Countries

Some countries have a unique symbol. Examples are the maple leaf for Canada, the kiwi bird for New Zealand, and the kangaroo for Australia.

The majority of countries in the world can be seen through several symbols. An example is India, which is seen through an elephant or an abstract symbol. Modern Egypt is represented by a pyramid, by a palm tree, or by an oval. Ancient Egypt is seen through a stylized Eye of Horus. All of these symbols can be seen on the next page.

States

States are represented by animal and bird symbols. A state can have more than one animal as a symbol, because the animals used to symbolize any state are the ones naturally found there. A flamingo, a heron, and an alligator all stand for Florida. A steer, a roadrunner bird, and an armadillo are signs of Texas.

India symbol

Pyramid

Areas

Areas of any country are represented by animal or bird figures which are found in that territory. For example, a seal can refer equally to Northern California, Alaska, and any area where seals live. A flying goose represents Canada as well as the cold states in the United States. A moose also stands for Canada and the northern United States. An elk, although properly found in Europe and Asia, is another symbol for a cold climate.

Palm tree

Why would we want to see all these places in the knuckles? Are we interested in various states, countries, and climates? Whether we are interested in them or not, these places can and do affect our lives, and have a role to play in them. Remember, the brain is interested in pointing out the influences of people and places in our lives. Designating places is what the symbols do.

Oval

Eye of Horus

How do we know what each symbol means? There are three types of symbols, according to their ease of interpretation. The first type, like the pyramid and kangaroo, has obvious symbolism. Other symbols can be understood through a general knowledge of the world and its climate.

Most people know enough to realize that elk do not run free in southern Florida, but alligators do. Or that seals do not flap about in Mississippi, but they do in Northern California, Alaska, and the Arctic Circle. Whatever knowledge you have of the world and its places can be used to interpret the symbols.

The second type of symbols relies on the wildlife of an area. Many more symbols exist than those mentioned in the short list in this chapter. Only the symbols which show up most often on knuckles are mentioned here.

The third type of symbol is the most exciting in its potential for research. It is also the least easily interpreted. This class of symbol is made up of certain shapes and designs which appear in the knuckles, but have no immediately clear meaning. An example is the symbol for Arizona.

Arizona symbol

How was this symbol found? The unique or abstract designs which stand for certain states were first found in the area of the knuckle that they represent. This symbol was found in the part of the knuckle that corresponds to Arizona, not just once but many times. Research with clients validated its use. And the symbol was easy to spot

New Mexico symbol

because a similar symbol had previously emerged in the New Mexico area of the knuckle.

This shape was clearly an abstract form of a mesa. A mesa defines the essence of New Mexico. Later on, the same mesa, but with the three vertical lines above it, was found in the Arizona area.

In summary, the three classes of interpretation developed so far include symbols with an obvious association and meaning, wildlife figures associated with a place, and abstract forms whose meanings have to be developed. All of you are invited to develop your own symbols' meaning, when you discover a new form in a certain area of the knuckle — and you try it out and find it works.

A Special Use of Birds and Fish

One more use of symbols remains to be mentioned. Very simple forms of birds and fish occur quite often. Nearly every set of hands will have a simple bird or fish in one of the knuckles. The fish occurs most frequently, followed by the bird. Either symbol, in its simplest form, has the unique meaning of *opportunity.*

This use of birds and fish in the knuckle is a special reflection of the primitive nature of the symbols. Think of what the catch of a fish or a bird meant to early people. That catch was an opportunity — to survive. Today, opportunity has a different meaning — to get ahead. Interpreting the fish and birds in a knuckle as opportunity symbols is a modern application of an old truth: survival or advancement means making the most of the resources we find.

*Simple
fish*

We instinctively remember the value fish and birds had for our ancestors in sayings floating around today: "A bird in the hand is worth two in the bush" ... "The fish that got away" ... "The big fish in a small pond."

The fish for opportunity looks like the illustration to the left. The bird is also very simple.

A special form of fish is a double fish, or two fish facing nose to nose.

*Simple
bird*

All fish and all birds mean an opportunity when they are found in the knuckles, each according to the finger they are on: in work, on the index finger; in finances, on the middle finger; in love and happiness, on the ring finger; and in negotiations, on the little finger.

*Double
fish*

The most compelling of the opportunity symbols is the double fish. This symbol means a "big catch," a big or unusual opportunity.

FINDING THE SYMBOLS

You are looking for pictures in the knuckles as you search for symbols. The lines will arrange themselves into certain shapes, allowing you to see an animal figure on one knuckle, a boat or bowl or tent on another knuckle, and perhaps one of the abstract symbols on yet another knuckle. At first, try to find one or two symbols in any one person's hands. When you get used to seeing them, you may find more than one or two per person.

The easiest way to proceed is to look for:

1. Bird and fish symbols

2. Other animals

3. Geometric and abstract deigns

Let's look at a few samples, what you might find, and how to interpret them.

1. An index finger with a fish symbol on it; a middle finger with a mountain symbol:

   New career opportunity; mountain areas are important to the person's finances.

2. A middle finger with a fish symbol; an index finger with a mountain symbol:

   Good financial prospects. Mountain areas holds good job opportunities.

3. Little finger with a moose symbol; ring finger with a kangaroo symbol:

   Personal acquaintance with Australia or someone who lives there. Holds negotiations in a cold climate.

4. Ring finger with a symbol for France; little finger with symbol for England (these symbols are found on page 284):

   This person has family in France and negotiations in England.

Let's look at these samples again, and add timing to the pictures:

1. Nondominant hand, fish on index tip knuckle; dominant hand, mountain on middle knuckle, middle finger:

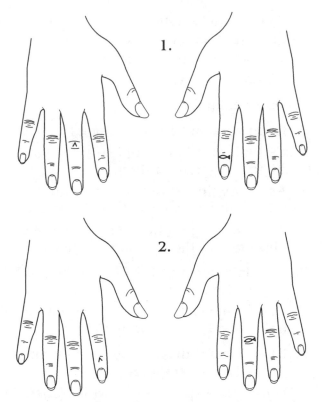

Career efforts from the last six months will bring a new opportunity within three years. In the present, there are financial prospects in mountain areas.

2. Nondominant hand, fish on middle knuckle of middle finger; dominant hand, mountain on index tip knuckle:

Financial groundwork done a year or more ago will pay off over the next three years, in increased opportunity. A mountain area will affect the career in six months to a year and a half.

3. Nondominant hand, moose on little finger, tip knuckle; dominant hand, kangaroo on ring finger, middle knuckle:

   Negotiations conducted in a cold climate six months ago will pay off over three years. Person currently knows someone in Australia or may travel there.

4. Nondominant hand, symbol for France on ring finger, tip knuckle; dominant hand, symbol for England on little finger, tip knuckle:

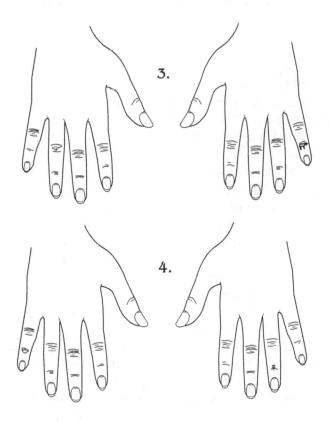

Family in France was important six months ago (maybe news of them was received), and will be important over the next three years. Negotiations will be conducted in England sometime during the next six to eighteen months.

These samples, especially those with the timing included, give you an idea how much information can be obtained from the symbols in the knuckles.

INTERPRETING THE SYMBOLS

First, look for fish and birds and apply their meaning of opportunity to the area of life the finger represents. If you wish, add the timing of the particular knuckle on which the symbol is found to give more precise information.

Next, look for animal figures, and decide what type of climate they are found in. Next see what area of the knuckle they are on. Use these two clues to decode the symbol's meaning, and apply it to the area of life the finger represents.

A bear in the middle knuckle of the middle fingers means financial dealings in a cold or woodsy area. A bear appearing in a knuckle refers to a cold climate. Now imagine the bear is located in the north central area of the knuckle: The bear will represent places like the northern states of Wisconsin or Minnesota.

Again, use the timing of the knuckle itself, if you want additional information.

Finally, look for any unusual shapes or designs. See if the abstract symbol is one of those from the list in this chapter. If it is, use that meaning. If it is not, take your first clue from the area of the knuckle on which the symbol is found.

As the client if he or she has any contact with the area highlighted in the knuckle by the presence of the symbol. For instance, a symbol in the northwest. Ask if the person knows anyone to the northwest. If the answer is yes, ask which state the people live in. Realize that the symbol represents that state for that person. For future use, make a note of the symbol and the state it represented, and see if the meaning is the same when you find the same symbol on another person.

COUNTRIES IDENTIFIED BY SYMBOLS

At this time, only a few countries have their own symbols. More are being developed, and you are invited to add your own experience to the files. Feel free to write the author with notes on what you find. If you have regular contact with South Korea, for instance, you may come up with a symbol for that country from your own hands or your family's hands.

Africa			Lion, Tiger
Australia			Kangaroo
Belize			Kangaroo (world's second largest coral reef is there)
Canada			Maple leaf, Flying goose
China			Kite with straight string

Country	Symbol	Description
Egypt	△ ♀ ⌒	Pyramid, Palm frond, Oval
England	∪	Shield
France	⊞ × ⊉	Shield with cross in it; X; Double flag with two squares
Germany	⋀ ⊓	Hut
Greece	⸸ ⸷ ⌒	Poseidon trident; fish
India	⊕ ⊗	Circle with cross or X
Iran	ⓐ	Peacock
Israel	Y	Y
Italy	⊓ ⊕	Double flag with curved sides; Maltese cross
Japan	♩	Kite with curved string
Mexico	🐂	Bull
New Zealand	🐦	Kiwi bird
Russia	⋀ ⅀	Letter M; Bear
Scandinavia	⌒	Viking ship
Scotland	⊢	Flag
South Africa	◇ ⋈	Diamond, Bow tie
Spain	🐂	Bull
Thailand	⬜	Flag
United States	🐓	Hen

STATES IDENTIFIED BY SYMBOLS

State	Symbol	Meaning
Alaska		Seal
Arizona		Mesa outline
California (North)		Seal
California (South)		Dolphin, or any large fish
Colorado		Tent
Florida		Flamingo
Hawaii		Snow-capped volcano
Louisiana		Alligator
Montana		Elk
New Mexico		Tent; Mesa outline
North Carolina		Small bird
Oregon		Elk
Tennessee		A soldier figure
Texas		Armadillo; Roadrunner
Washington		Elk
Wyoming		Bear

Check for animal symbols connected with a certain climate; an elk means any cold climate. An alligator means a warm climate. Big fish, like porpoises and sharks, mean an area where an ocean is found. Such fish can represent either coast or the Gulf of Mexico.

OTHER ERAS OF HISTORY OR CULTURES IDENTIFIED BY SYMBOLS

Another fascinating development in the world of knuckles is the appearance of symbols denoting ancient people and cultures, or bygone eras of history.

Ancient Egypt		Eye of Horus
Ancient Greece		Porpoise, or big fish
Ancient India		Temple
Ancient Israel (Hebrews)		Bowl on a stand
Atlantis		Cross with a long vertical line and shorter arms
Aztecs		Cross with wider arms
Crusades		Double flag, 2 flags not same height
Incas		Cross with wider arms
Mayans		Cross with wider arms
Native Americans		Large X, with base connected
Phoenicians		Stylized boat, like a bowl

TYPES OF ANIMAL SYMBOLS

In theory, any animal in existence can show up in the knuckles. However, a few seem to repeat themselves. Here is a list of the most frequently found symbols.

Birds: All kinds of birds exist in the knuckles, and they serve one of two purposes: either as a symbol of opportunity, and in this case the bird is drawn very simply; or as a distinct symbol of a place. Birds in this category are, as examples, ducks, eagles, flamingos, geese, herons, roadrunners, robins, sea gulls, swans, and woodpeckers.

Cats: Domestic and wild, particularly cougars, jaguars, lions, panthers, and tigers.

Dogs: Domestic, large and small. Occasionally the form will be distinct, revealing a German shepherd or a Scottish terrier. But mostly the symbols divide into "large" and "small" dogs.

Fish: Any number of fish, large and small, show up. The large fish in particular take on different, distinct forms, such as barracudas, porpoises, sharks, and whales.

The fish appears either as a single fish, or as a double fish, with the noses touching as they face each other. This is a separate symbol meaning opportunity.

Wild animals: Deer, elk, moose, and in particular, bears. An image of "Smokey the Bear" has been found in the Wyoming area of the knuckle and represents Yellowstone Park, as well. All of the larger wild animals are meant to represent areas located in cooler climates.

One small creature: Very rarely, a tiny creature that is highly symbolic shows up — a rat! A rat is found with human beings, and is a cartoon figure which acts as a stand-in for a real life person, whose qualities are just what you might imagine — those of a rat. A rat in a knuckle is a warning signal.

INITIALS

At this time, four initials from our alphabet have been found in knuckles relatively often. The four initials are A, D, K, and M. These letters stand for names of people, places, and even of businesses. Their purpose is to help identify people and places seen in the knuckles. Each initial can represent a male or female first name, a last name, or a city. As an example, A can stand for Andrea or Andrew or Atlanta, or even a business, Atlas Tire Company.

K is interesting because it has been found to represent a hard C sound, as in the name Cook, as well as words beginning with K, like Kevin.

These four letters are the first initials of a name, with one exception.

A can be used for a name whose whole sound depends on that A, like Jane, or Dave; or in a name made up of mostly A's, like Amanda.

When you find an initial and use it to help identify a person — "who do you know in the South whose name begins with M" — you will be a hit. To your own satisfaction, the initial is a great shortcut, and not ambiguous. Initials help narrow the field in the process of identification. Of course your client will think you are psychic, if the initial fits. But in fact you can find these four letters in the knuckle. Labeling through initials is another efficient way the knuckles work.

At this point, we are going to wind down the presentation of warriors, cartoon figures, and symbols in the knuckles. These three types taken together are the "lines" of the knuckles. Their role is very important — crucial, in fact — in gaining in-depth information about a person's life. However, they are not the only source of information, and it is strongly suggested that you work first with shape and color as a background to the study of the lines. Perhaps a couple of weeks or a month at first should be devoted to the shape and color — and as a not entirely facetious note — the rest of your life to the study of the lines! Of course, the ideal way is to combine all three factors — color, shape, and lines — and to use their placement in each knuckle to understand each area of life and its timing.

Shape and color are more limited in their application, and their forms are not as diverse as the lines. The shape of your knuckles talks about your experience and how it has affected you. The color of your knuckles reveals your momentum for the future. But when we come to the lines, we open Pandora's Box — in the sense that lines represent someone other than ourselves, a whole range of people; or places, in the case of symbols. The diversity represented by the lines is never-ending.

CASE HISTORY

The secret of the back of the hands and the knuckles has been hinted at often in these pages — the world of the back of the hands is our world with the people in it. We carry a record of our interaction with the world in a most immediate form. To be connected with the world this way and with people we know and love, by carrying representative images of them in our knuckles, we are living expressions of the fact that we are all connected!

The connection between all of us is so vital that the images in our knuckles are constantly being updated. That is not all. Even more startling is the fact that our own palms do not contain all the pieces of the puzzle of our lives.

As an analogy, if your energy field were represented by one hundred marbles, ninety-five of them would be found in one place, and the remaining five scattered among other places. This is a way of saying that not all of the information about your life is in your hands, but in some else's hands. This is the secret to knuckles and their world! To know yourself best, you must interact with others.

And to receive information about yourself and your future, you need not only consult someone about your own knuckles, but you can send family members to the same practitioner to check out some of your prospects. That is because their hands will often have certain pieces of information about you that your own knuckles do not have. And this works in reverse, too. Much information is found in your knuckles about others, including certain "exclusives," pieces of information about them that even they do not have in their own knuckles.

An example of how this interdependent information occurs is seen in the following story.

A client once came to have a look at all her prospects for the future. She was a professional woman, happy in her job, and worked well with others in the office. The coworkers were all friendly and interested in each others' welfare.

On this client's first index knuckle, the middle knuckle which gives background information, one figure stood out — a girl who was represented by a fully drawn or cartoon figure. She was a young co-worker, symbolized by the fact she had on a short skirt. But the striking point is that the short skirt allowed a view of the top of her legs, and the left leg was sketchily drawn at the outside, near the upper thigh. To make matters more interesting, there was an initial A drawn clearly above her head.

I told the woman I saw in her knuckle the outline of a young girl with an initial "A," which was possibly a clue to her name. And that the woman had something wrong with her left leg.

My question was, could she place such a woman in her work environment, and if so, did this woman ever injure her leg? A car wreck? Fall off a horse? The client disclaimed any such knowledge. Without an answer to the questions, I went on to the next figures and interpretation of her knuckles.

Once the reading was finished, she looked at me and said quietly, "You know that young woman you saw at first? The one with the injured leg? That's Andrea. I work with her. She has multiple sclerosis and her left leg bothers her most of all."

Because the color on the knuckle surrounding the figure was good, I told my client that this young woman would recover from some of her symptoms and difficulty.

The client in turn, unknown to me, took the story back to Andrea at the office.

Many months later, an older woman came to see me. She did not seem to have any particular questions, or even much interest in the whole process, until we got to the ring finger on her right hand. There in the middle knuckle was an image of a sinking ship, with a lighthouse in the background.

Having worked some years with the knuckles' symbols, I knew enough to realize her knuckle, especially a ring finger knuckle, connected as it is with family and loved ones, did not have a picture of a real ship on it.

Furthermore, the coloring around the sinking ship image was not good, so I suspected ill health. And for a female member of the family purely because an ocean and ship are both feminine. That was taking subtlety a step forward. But the approach worked. As I asked her, "Do you have a woman in the family whose health you are worried about?" she dissolved into tears, saying, "Yes! That's why I came here. The only reason I came here. I had to know. The sick person is my daughter, Andrea, and you saw her in a coworker's hands some months ago. I want to know what is going to happen to her."

Her tears cleared up when I assured her that her daughter would recover from her symptoms, or go into remission, because the lighthouse in the background had several horizontal lines, like rays of light, coming from the lighthouse window. In fact, Andrea did get better.

This is an example of how information got into the knuckles of two different people, a coworker and a mother of a girl I never met. But at a distance I was able to predict a positive future outcome to her immediate poor health. This happened because both the friend and the mother knew, at a subconscious level, that Andrea would get better, and the knuckles printed out the reality.

The emotional impact for a mother of hearing twice, and in a blind test at that, that her daughter would improve, put her at ease.

Analysis

Andrea appeared on the middle index finger knuckle on the nondominant hand of her friend. That means the image referred to ill health for her for a year or more. In fact, her condition had gone on for a couple of years. But the nondominant hand also shows a future of up to three years ahead. The prediction from the friend's finger was better health for Andrea, within three years.

Andrea then appeared on her mother's ring finger, middle knuckle, on the dominant hand. The time frame for that knuckle is the present. And at the time the woman sat with me, her daughter did still have problems. The reassurance offered by the lighthouse image did not have a future time frame, only a promise with no particular time in the future specified. But using the information from the co-worker's knuckle, we knew that within three years, at the most, Andrea would be better.

This is an example of how "one marble," or piece of the puzzle, appeared in a friend's hand, and "another marble," or piece of information, appeared in her mother's hand. A most interesting study would have been the opportunity to study Andrea's own hands — which would have "ninety-five marbles," or most of the relevant information about the future.

Working with knuckles on any level, whether on a "first person" basis or for someone at a distance, reveals much of the mystery of life and the dynamics that affect all of us, in our lives and our loves.

Learning all about the knuckles takes a little work, but it is work that is amply rewarded. The fun of this new system, once you have the basics in place, is its flexibility. One image can refer to more than one person. One symbol can stand for more than one place. This very openness and potential for expansion is what lets the subject — and its benefits — grow.

If you choose to concentrate only on shape and color in the knuckles, you still receive a world of information. You can use as many or as few details as you like, and still be a good "knuckle interpreter." Only time and practice will let each individual find a comfortable level of expression with the material.

The important point is that hands are still rewarding us with a knowledge about ourselves and our world. This system, in its figures, symbols, and emphasis on place-in-the-world, shares an orientation with the most ancient concerns of humanity, depicted from earliest days in art and legends.

The elemental form the images take brings us back to prehistory, and brings us close to native people and cultures who were guardians of the earth and the world as they knew it. And the images just as capably inform us about our world today.

A recent letter from St. Joseph's Indian School in Chamberlain, South Dakota, had this logo on their stationery.

The arrows and obvious depiction of the four corners of the world come close to the reality of the knuckles' imagery — too close to be an accident. Most interesting of all was the large logo on the envelope which follows.

A very arresting image! Animals in the four quarters of the world, alive with a meaning and message for those who can decode it. Like the primitive images in the knuckles, this image can be instinctively understood. The simplicity of the lines and images and their concentration on the heart of life and the soul of the world makes them come alive.

PRIMITIVE NATURE OF
THE SYMBOLS

The primitive nature of the images in the knuckles is striking. Taken together, the images present life at its most basic level: people and their world, people in their world. The imagery is simple but profound. The quest we have had since our first days on earth, finding a way to fit in our environment and flourish, is at the core of the knuckles' images. This is why their message is powerful and touches the heart and soul of anyone who has the experience of dwelling on and decoding the images in their knuckles.

The images speak to the nature of humanity in a natural setting. Oceans, sky, and mountains form a backdrop, and nearly all the movement shown in the knuckles is represented through "foot power," on foot, on horseback (and other load-bearing animals), and on boats.

The images are archetypal, and often straight out of fairy tales. Flying carpets represent another mode of travel in this context. Dress takes on all the ancient magic of a Turkish costume, a knight and his lady, or a German burgher from the sixteenth century.

At this time, imagery in the knuckles does not directly correspond to today's reality, in terms of physical structures. There are no skyscrapers, no heaped up piles of buildings, or freeways with cars snaking down them. There are no ranch houses, no mansions, and not even a suggestion of the amenities we have today — the local grocery store, pharmacy, drive-in medical clinics, gas stations, or department stores.

This fact does not discount today's reality. It would seem that the knuckles' imagery is a time-honored guide, addressing our basic needs, that will help us all deal with the development of our lives in our modern settings. The rules are the same as they have always been: survival, care and love for another person, the creation of children, the passing of one generation into another.

While the imagery speaks to the essential nature and needs of everyone today, there is perhaps another reason for the primitive nature of the images. The part of the brain that is printing out these images is ancient, and only knows such symbols as people, animals, physical places, and necessities such as implements to shape a world, early forms of housing, and a touch from other eras of history. This makes the images more touching and eloquent, even sacred, as a way of getting in touch with ourselves at a deep level.

The knuckles' imagery can be a fountain of inspiration in our quest to build a better world for ourselves today, by keeping us in touch with basic reality. Eternal guidance and wisdom is the gift of the knuckles.

20 Putting the Pieces Together

Working with the knuckles involves using the elements we have covered chapter by chapter. Four pieces of the puzzle must be understood before we begin to interpret the shape, color, and lines in the knuckles. These four pieces are the meaning of the hands, the meaning of the knuckles, the meaning of the fingers, and timing for the knuckles.

Nondominant Hand

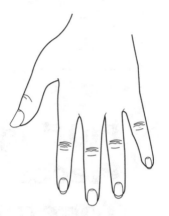

Background information on issues of a year or more ago, and an overview of events of the last six months. Both of these influence the next three years.

This hand's role is to describe our lives.

Dominant Hand

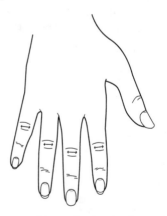

Information on the present circumstances and on their outcome within six to eighteen months.

This hand describes events and people and the role they will play in our future.

First Set of Knuckles

Middle knuckles on nondominant hand.

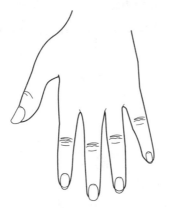

These knuckles provide background information on any issue of a year or more ago that will affect the future within three years.

Second Set of Knuckles

Tip knuckles on nondominant hand.

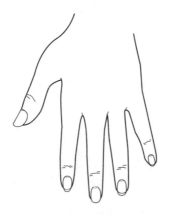

These knuckles provide information about the conditions and people in our lives within the last six months that will affect our future within three years.

Third Set of Knuckles

Middle knuckles on dominant hand.

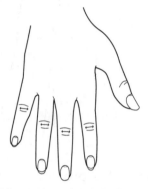

These knuckles provide information about present conditions and people in our lives that will affect our future within a year and a half.

Fourth Set of Knuckles

Tip knuckles on dominant hand.

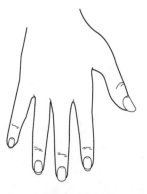

These knuckles reveal the outcome of issues and concerns covered in the three previous sets of knuckles, within six to eighteen months.

Meaning of the Fingers

Index finger	Career
Middle finger	Money
Ring finger	Love and friendship
Little finger	Deal-making ability (negotiations)

Timing for the Knuckles

Set 1	Past: 1 year ago.
	Future: Up to 3 years. Anytime from now to 3 years ahead.
Set 2	Past: 6 months ago.
	Future: Anytime up to 3 years ahead.
Set 3	Present: 2 months ago and 2 months ahead.
Set 4	Future: 6 months ahead at the knuckle. 18 months ahead at the fingertip.

Knuckle Shapes, Colors, and Lines

Shape	**Key Meaning**
Smooth	Life is easy.
Raised	Experience in the world.

Shape	Key Meaning
Raised and firm	High profile in the world; very experienced.
Raised and soft	Indecision. Experience has been difficult.
Dented	Pressures and stress.
Furrowed	Effort that has not been rewarded or paid a good return. Life needs more balance.

Color	Key Meaning
Pink area on white knuckle	Positive momentum. Success on the way.
Shiny area on dark knuckle	Positive momentum. Success on the way.
Pale area on white knuckle	Negative momentum. Challenges ahead.
Darker/dull area on dark knuckle	Negative momentum. Challenges ahead.

Warriors: Stick figures who tell a story by their posture.

Cartoon figures: Fully drawn figures who tell a story by their profile and dress and the way they are grouped together.

Symbols: Designs and animal figures that give clues to geographical areas (countries, states) and individual states and countries.

Let's build a few examples, using these pieces of the puzzle.

Dominant hand	Shape	Smooth
Index finger	Color	Pink
Middle knuckle	Figure	Warrior in victory posture

Meaning: The person's career has gone well (smooth shape), and this fact makes the person expect good results in his career. Right now (middle knuckle on dominant hand) career prospects are excellent (pink color, warrior in victory posture).

Dominant hand	Shape	Smooth
Index finger	Color	White
Middle knuckle	Figure	Warrior in victory posture

Meaning: The person's career has gone well, and this fact makes the person expect good results in his career. Right now, however, a few challenging conditions have come up at work (white color), but everything will work out well (warrior in victory posture).

Dominant hand	Shape	Smooth
Index finger	Color	Pink
Middle knuckle	Figure	Warrior in defeat posture

Meaning: The person's career has gone well, and this fact makes the person expect good results in his or her career. Conditions are helpful, in general (pink color), but a problem could arise with a coworker or boss (warrior in defeat posture). This is what the person has to watch for in the present.

Dominant hand	Shape	Dented
Index finger	Color	Pink
Middle knuckle	Figure	Warrior in victory posture

Meaning: Although past pressures have conditioned this person to respond to his or her career as a stressful situation, current conditions are excellent.

Dominant hand	Shape	Furrowed
Index finger	Color	Pink
Middle knuckle	Figure	Warrior in victory posture

Meaning: Although this person has not recently been rewarded for his efforts at work (furrowed shape), he stands to get some good news in his career shortly (present knuckle, pink color, victorious warrior).

Dominant hand	Shape	Furrowed
Index finger	Color	White
Middle knuckle	Figure	Warrior in victory posture

Meaning: Although the person has not gotten satisfaction and rewards for his or her efforts recently, and although challenging conditions prevail at work right now, help is on the way. A boss or co-worker will be of assistance.

Nondominant hand	Shape	Smooth
Index finger	Color	Pink
Middle knuckle	Figure	Warrior in victory posture

Meaning: Conditions for a year or more at work have been smooth. Whatever the person has accomplished over the last year (pink color) will pay off shortly. Bosses and coworkers are going to be helpful over the next three years.

Nondominant hand	Shape	Furrowed
Index finger	Color	White
Middle knuckle	Figure	Warrior in victory posture

Meaning: Conditions for a year or more at work have been depressing. The person has not received much reward for his or her efforts, and the challenge of the situation (white color) will continue by and large for awhile. But before three years are up (nondominant hand's future time frame), the person will have help (victorious warrior) and better career conditions.

For every example we have just looked at, you can substitute the middle finger, and make the subject money; substitute the ring finger for the index, make the subject love, and the warrior refers to a partner or friend; and substitute the little finger for the index, and read it for negotiations, how they have fared, and what to expect in the future.

Notice how the shape and color modify the meaning of the knuckle, and how important the posture of the warrior figure is.

This is the beginning way to interpret a knuckle on any finger. Practice doing this for awhile before you add the element of geography. When you are comfortable working with the knuckles' shape, color, and lines as an indication of a "bottom-line" future, along with the accompanying past and present conditions, then you can branch out and concentrate on interpreting figures in any one area of the knuckle, or the color of any one area of the knuckle.

When you are ready, use the examples above, and simply specify where the warrior is found.

Dominant hand	Shape	Furrowed
Index finger	Color	White
Middle knuckle	Figure	Warrior in victory posture, northeast area of knuckle

Meaning: The same as in our last example, with the additional detail that help will come from someone located in the northeast.

If you can name a state or a country for the figure, you are really skilled. You would name a state if the area under the victorious warrior were pink and corresponded to a state. This means the pink would just cover the figure. A larger area of pink would most likely cover an area, like the northeast. If a symbol, like a kangaroo, accompanied the victorious warrior figure, you would tell your client, using the above example, that help will come from someone in Australia.

You can also substitute a cartoon figure for the warrior and read it for dress, profile, and grouping: add a later location, just as we saw above for the warrior figure.

Please work with the basics. As is true with any new art or science, you will find that you like some parts better than others, or that certain aspects of the subject will come more easily. Concentrate on those parts at first. You may choose to stay with those elements that appeal to you or make sense to you, and not push to do a thoroughly detailed analysis of each knuckle.

The point of this system is to enjoy finding new information in a brand new territory, and a little bit goes a long way in entertainment value and in helping you deduce the future. Good luck!

Remember, this is a developing art/science, and if you like it, and choose to work with it, you will be one of a handful of pioneers helping further a new area of knowledge meant to benefit many people and expand the horizons of one of the most wonderful, magical, and practical subjects we know ... the world of the hands.

On the following pages you will find listed, with their current prices, some of the books now available on related subjects. Your book dealer stocks most of these and will stock new titles in the Llewellyn series as they become available. We urge your patronage.

TO GET A FREE CATALOG

To obtain our full catalog, you are invited to write (see address below) for our bi-monthly news magazine/catalog, *Llewellyn's New Worlds of Mind and Spirit*. A sample copy is free, and it will continue coming to you at no cost as long as you are an active mail customer. Or you may subscribe for just $10 in the United States and Canada ($20 overseas, first class mail). Many bookstores also have *New Worlds* available to their customers. Ask for it.

TO ORDER BOOKS AND TAPES

If your book store does not carry the titles described on the following pages, you may order them directly from Llewellyn by sending the full price in U.S. funds, plus postage and handling (see below).

Credit card orders: VISA, MasterCard, American Express are accepted. Call toll-free within the USA and Canada at 1-800-THE-MOON.

Special Group Discount: Because there is a great deal of interest in group discussion and study of the subject matter of this book, we offer a 20% quantity discount to group leaders or agents. Our Special Quantity Price for a minimum order of five copies of *The New Palmistry* is $51.80 cash-with-order. Include postage and handling charges noted below.

Postage and Handling: Include $4 postage and handling for orders $15 and under; $5 for orders *over* $15. There are no postage and handling charges for orders over $100. Postage and handling rates are subject to change. We ship UPS whenever possible within the continental United States; delivery is guaranteed. Please provide your street address as UPS does not deliver to P.O. boxes. Orders shipped to Alaska, Hawaii, Canada, Mexico and Puerto Rico will be sent via first class mail. Allow 4-6 weeks for delivery. **International orders:** Airmail – add retail price of each book and $5 for each non-book item (audiotapes, etc.); Surface mail – add $1 per item.

Minnesota residents add 7% sales tax.

Mail orders to:
Llewellyn Worldwide
P.O. Box 64383-K352, St. Paul, MN 55164-0383, U.S.A.

For customer service, call (612) 291-1970.

PALMISTRY
The Whole View
by Judith Hipskind
Here is a unique approach to palmistry! Judy Hipskind
not only explains how to analyze hands, but also
explains why hand analysis works. The approach is
based on a practical rationale and is easy to understand.
Over 130 illustrations accompany the informal, positive
view of hand analysis.

This new approach to palmistry avoids categorical predictions and presents the meaning of the palm as a syn-
thesis of many factors: the shape, gestures, flexibility,
mounts and lives of each hand—as well as a combination of the effects of both heredity and the environment.
No part of the hand is treated as a separate unit; the
hand reflects the entire personality. An analysis based
on the method presented in this book is a rewarding
experience for the client—a truly whole view!
0-87542-306-X, 248 pgs., 5-1/4 x 8, illus., $8.95

PALMASCOPE
The Instant Palm Reader
by Linda Domin

The road of your life is mapped out on the palm of your hand. When you know how to interpret the information, it is like seeing an aerial view of all the scenes of your life that you will travel. You will get candid, uplifting revelations about yourself: personality, childhood, career, finances, family, love life, talents and destiny. Author Linda Domin has upgraded and modernized the obsolete substance of palmistry. By decoding all the palm-lines systems of the major schools of palmistry and integrating them with her own findings, she has made it possible for anyone to assemble a palm reading that can be trusted for its accuracy.

This book was specifically designed to answer those personal questions unanswerable by conventional methods. Using this exciting method of self-discovery, you can now uncover your hidden feelings and unconscious needs as they are etched upon the palm of your hand.
0-87542-162-8, 256 pgs., 7 x 10, illus., $12.95

REVEALING HANDS
How to Read Palms
by Richard Webster

Palmistry has been an accurate tool for self-knowledge and prediction for thousand of years. The ability to read palms can lead you to a better understanding of yourself, as well as the complex motivations of other people. Guide and advise others in a sensitive and caring manner, determine compatibility between couples, and help people decide what type of career suits them best.

Revealing Hands makes it is easier than ever to learn the science of palmistry. As soon as you complete the first chapter, you can begin reading palms with confidence and expertise. Professional palmist and teacher Richard Webster leads you step-by-step through the subject with clear explanations and life-size hand drawings that highlight the points being covered. He provides sample scripts that can serve as a foundation for your readings for others, and he answers all of the questions he has been asked by his students over the years. Whether you are interested in taking up palmistry professionally or just for fun, you will find the information in this book exceptionally entertaining and easy to use.

0-87542-870-3, 300 pgs., 7 x 10, 117 illus., $12.95